TWELVE + ONE

Some Jo'burg poets:
their artistic lives and poetry

Interviewed by **Mike Alfred**

Published by

Botsotso
Box 30952
Braamfontein
2017

botsotso@artslink.co.za
www.botsotso.org.za

ISBN 978-0-9814205-3-0

We would like to thank the National Arts Council of South Africa
for its assistance in publishing this book.

NATIONAL ARTS COUNCIL
OF SOUTH AFRICA

Editor: Allan Kolski Horwitz

Cover, layout, design and graphics: Vivienne Preston

Contents

Interviews by Mike Alfred

Introduction

I conceived this work because most poets living around the corner in Johannesburg, as is their poetry, are largely ignored. Academe, intent upon the 'classics', ignores contemporary South African poetry. Publishers won't touch it because the financial rewards are sparse; those few collections published by courageous small journals are seldom reviewed by the mainstream press. Different poet groupings, inheritors of the South African political scene, remain aloof, even unknown to one another. Our literature-ignorant population is not in any way, enticed to read poetry. But despite the paucity of recognition and reward, poets are never still, they create, they persevere, they refuse few invitations to dance with the muse, they fight a never ending battle to perform and to get published; poetry is a true art form. My intention then, was to give our local, neglected poets, a 'louder' voice.

My approach was to interview eleven Joburg poets of all descriptions, then transcribe those interactions into word pictures of the poetic life. As it turned out, thirteen poets are here presented, I being the thirteenth, because Allan Kolski Horwitz [the publisher], as we were putting the book together, insisted on interviewing me ["so you think you can stay aloof?"]. Additionally, he wanted to include a young woman poet who gives a lot of insight into the burgeoning Spoken Word scene. In extension to the transcribed interviews, we asked our so cooperative respondents to provide us with four or five poems together with an explanation of why and how they came to be written. As such, this is a book about poets, their artistic lives and their poetry.

The poets were not chosen at random; several are known to me and several were known to the publisher. Several are recognized in various poetic undergrounds. Several more were recommended by our early interviewees. In terms of colour and gender, this is a broadly representative 'quota'. All the poets have something to say, all are fine craftspeople, but this small book is not to be seen as a meritocratic and exclusive collection. I could have filled the pages with the equally fascinating stories and work of many other artists.

I suppose I shouldn't find it strange that most people don't read or enjoy poetry. School, an antediluvian institution so entirely useless at motivating young people, is the worst place to inculcate a love of poetry. After being driven to mindlessly rote-learn the poetry of bygone ages without the benefit of either historical or biographical context, adolescents emerge not only indifferent, but with complete determination to never approach a poem again. Somehow the celebrity struck world believes that if a writer is not of the time-entrenched, popular stature of Tennyson, Keats, Whitman, etc., then they're not worth considering. The idols are worshipped and good contemporary poetry is needlessly dismissed.

It seems to me that present day poetry, written by people called Siphiwe or Gail or Ahmed, rather than Shakespeare or Eliot, is just the thing for our world: contemporary poetry is short, it's sharp, sad, funny, politically trenchant, sociologically and historically relevant. It pines for lost love, mourns dead parents, describes the landscape, expresses a wonder for childhood, explores the meaning of life, all in magical language. It's so convenient; how else might you read a novel in three verses, a whole biography spread over just two-and-a-half pages. Where else are you likely to be subjected to thirty different voices in a single publication. Poetry is perfect for our frenetic world, but no one's discovered or acknowledged it yet. A small, slip-into-your–pocket journal is a Gautrain or taxi journey's entertainment or a laughing, quietly tearful, thought provoking flight companion.

Transcribing the recorded interviews was hard but rewarding work. I felt very close to the poets. With the machine, I could stop them and start them talking. I could contemplate their messages, but very seldom did I alter their words and never their intent. All the respondents edited their own interviews with the request that they modify only factual inaccuracies and incorrect naming. Listening, I could hear their intonations, their hesitations and strong assertions. I regretted that it was difficult to define their emotions upon the page. On tape they came alive, they were talking only to me and their story was unique. I suggest that you read their words with a consciousness of the feelings behind the experiences. One generalization that emerged from their lives in poetry, is that nearly all were captivated by the word from an early age. Several were helped to read before the age of five, before going to school. Many loved the children's Classics read at bedtime by parents. Some were denied true literature when young but somehow were stimulated by cowboy and detective pulp fiction read by family members. Some had to wait for a good English teacher to set them aflame. That seemed to be sufficient for a lifelong creation of good, expressive writing.

So here is a small book about poetry, spoken and written by your Johannesburg city neighbours. Of course, artists are living and creating in other centres too. Would you believe that we live in an undiscovered, treasure vein, featuring contemporary life in the 21st Century. All you need to do is spend a few rand, open a slim book and read with an open mind. Perhaps you also need to embarrass your local bookseller into stocking some here-and-now poetry books. Milton is all very well, but he won't expire if you don't read him and his reputation is anyway assured. The literary power mongers have been withholding our poetic riches far too long. Here's a message: poetry is readily available, demand it. Enjoy its entertainment and education, know how earnestly local poets are attempting to communicate with you.

Mike Alfred
Johannesburg

Jane Fox

From the motorway, I take the off ramp to arrive a few minutes later at JF's compact dwelling in large grounds, part of an original farm house in a once bucolic Rivonia. I'm greeted by a trim, strong striding, feisty, seventy-something Jane, and Sirius, her one-year old German Shepherd who sticks his nose where he might not if he were human. We've known each other for some years but not well. Jane is Lionel Abrahams' widow. Lionel helped me enormously when I first started writing poetry. I wrote a biographical essay about him in my *Johannesburg Portraits*. Exchanging pleasantries we pass through the familiar and welcoming house to sit on the quiet patio where our conversation and Jane's story unfolds.

I kid Jane about the alacrity with which she agreed to be interviewed for this series. Jane responds. 'I suppose that any validation that I am a poet, is wonderful. I've always thought that poetry is something I do on the side. Serious writing for me is prose, so if I can be thought of as a poet too, that's wonderful. That's what I've been doing these last three years, only poetry, but I've recently started writing another play.' Knowing that this is a powerful and very real issue with many poets, I pursue, 'Why do you need validation?' Jane [chuckling], 'I suppose I have a deep seated inferiority complex lurking in the corner somewhere.' 'Pardon me if I brush that aside,' I say, knowing few women so held together, strong and confident.

We pass on to one of Jane's particular poems. I say, 'I love, above all your other poems, that wonderful sonnet; the sonnet about Lionel, your love and your mourning. If anything would say to me that you are a poet that would say it.'

ON SEEING DAWN OVER THE VLEI
AT WAYLANDS FARM

> As when a swallow darts across the lake
> dipping to catch mid-flight a floating fly,
> the bird and its reflection move as one:
> two pairs of wings, two flights, one pattern make.
> The bird above lives, breathes, will one day die;
> its copy waits below, life hath it none.
> So I, earth-shackled, in suspension be
> till thou, my heart, dip earthward in thy flight
> and kiss thy mirrored image on my face.
> Thus thine on mine imprinted wilt thou see,
> and as thou risest up through heaven's light
> with stronger wings to draw me too to grace,
> although at first it seemed that thou didst die –
> in clearer light thou art more real than I.

Jane says, 'I suppose it's the one I am most pleased with. I don't often try to write something in a formal mode and it worked and I still think it works. Actually, I had another look at it this morning because it's being published in Patricia Schonstein's anthology, *Africa! my Africa!*, along with a whole lot of other poets. So I think that after all these years it still works for me and makes me feel slightly lumpish in the throat.'

'Would you like to talk about your relationship with Lionel?'

'Mm, it's quite hard to characterise,' says Jane. 'The strange thing is that I have always, from a child, thought that my perfect life would be to be involved with somebody who would in some way be needing something special from me that other people couldn't give and who was himself a writer of some kind. This is because books have always been my whole life. I taught myself to read at the age of about four, I couldn't wait for school, I had to do it then and there. And I always had this airy, romantic idea of a genius who was in some way, I don't think I ever went as far as to say handicapped, but in some way needful, needing me.

'I met Lionel through a mutual friend. It was a very extraordinary meeting. Lionel had a niece called Lulu and she lived in a flat in Braamfontein next door to my best friend, who happened to be a homoeopathic doctor. Lionel was not recovering from a spinal op very well so Lulu said to Paula, my friend – do you think homeopathy might help, would you at least come and talk to him? Paula went to see Lionel. She came straight back from that meeting and she came to see me, and said, I have met the man for you! At that time I was married and had three children in their late teenage and early twenties. So, I said, oh yes, who? Nice? And she said he's a poet called Lionel Abrahams. I said, oh yes, I have read a couple of his poems, I know who he is. She then lent me a copy of his autobiographical stories, *The Celibacy of Felix Greenspan*. And I thought, bugger this, I have to go and meet this man, I have to. So after three weeks of not quite daring to dial the number, I dialed his number and he sounded kind of detached but friendly and he said, well ja, so you're a friend of Paula's, I'd like to meet you. So I went and met him one evening. I intended to stay an hour and I ended up leaving at about half-past-eleven that night. We talked and talked, and I came home thinking 'this is the man I want to spend my life with.' I went to see him frequently thereafter and let him know in no uncertain terms that that was how I felt about him. Poor guy, he didn't have a hope. I was so determined. And I think that neither of us ever regretted it.

'I got divorced, which was only a rubber stamping of something that had happened long before. My husband and I hadn't really been communicating for a long time.'

Jane first came to South Africa when she was twenty-five.

'During the war we lived just outside London, we were very heavily involved in the blitz. We were bombed out of our house at one stage. But it was a kind of way of life. I experienced the war years between four and ten. You don't question things between four and ten: that's just how life is. You get used to coming downstairs in your dressing gown every night when there's an air raid. We were bombed out right at the end of the war by one of those V2 rockets, the unmanned flying bombs that came over.'

I ask, 'Did the war have any effect on you later?'

'I'm terribly glad to have experienced it. It was at a time when England was proud of what she was doing; there was a certain gritty determination to hang on no matter what. And I think all of us who were there then inherited a bit of that determination. It is a kind of inheritance, which may sound crazy.' 'It doesn't sound crazy,' I respond, and we end up by agreeing that Winston Churchill, *Time* magazine's 'Man of the Century', was the epitome of British war-time courage. In Jane's words, 'He may have had, as has come out since, he may have had his down side, but I think he was the absolutely right person, at the right moment in the right place, and we probably would not have had such a good result without him; it might have gone the other way.'

Jane claims that her British attitudes and pride were not all that acceptable when she moved to SA in the sixties. 'I was surprised to find that we were so unpopular. It didn't do to say that you were English. Perhaps that's putting it a little strongly but suddenly I saw the other side of us, as resented colonialists.' I ask how she feels about living in SA now. 'I'd never leave! I've made a wonderful life for myself here. Hopefully I visit England once a year to see the friends, but I have no desire to go back and live there, because England has changed. It is not the same place. The country is still the same country and I love it, it's my home earth. Especially the countryside, because where we lived as I grew up we were near enough to the country to be a village still. To go to church on a Sunday and to go to school, I had to travel through fields and woods even though we were only twenty miles away from London; yes, they were English fields and English woods.

'No, I couldn't live there. The towns have become incredibly cosmopolitan. You could just as well be in Johannesburg as in Oxford St, London. It's become a Nanny State. You can't do anything. Here, you are free to make your own or break your own. In England you're not allowed to.' I ask whether she's perturbed by our politics. 'Well, I'd be pretty stupid not to be,' she bangs back. 'But I don't see that there's a great deal I can do about it. I'm not a political animal, I don't join parties, I don't join marches. In fact the word 'politics' makes me say thank you very much, but it's for somebody else not for me. I do obviously vote in elections as I believe it's everyone's duty to do so. I have a South African passport. As soon as the government changed I took out SA citizenship. I thought that was the right thing to do because I live here. This is my home as much as England is my home.'

'When and why did you start writing?'

'I have no idea why I started writing it. I've always messed about with writing, since a child. I was always top in the class with essays and such. It always came very easily to me. I was lucky to have parents who told me stories and gave me books which were beautifully written. *The Wind in the Willows* being the one that immediately leaps to mind. And I was given that when I was very young. I think it kind of shaped my ability with language. For me language is tremendously easy and language is what I really care about. I can't bear the way the media are slaughtering English – every advert that you get bombarded with for example – anyway that's a hobby horse.

'I started writing poetry seriously, not because I consciously decided that I

9

was going to, but I came to see it as a way of preserving something. If you have a transcendent experience of some kind or something that really hits you right there, you want in some way to keep it. The best way is to put it either in words, or music, or painting, or whatever it is you do; which is how I came to start writing poetry I suppose, although it was an unconscious start. You have something you really want to keep, to guard, to express, and maybe somebody else will read it and say, *I felt like that*. Poetry for me is distilled feeling.'

I say, 'But poetry is also a desire to share with others.'

'Yes, but if nobody reads it, tough titty. I don't do it to show to other people necessarily. It's very nice if someone says – wow, that's marvelous – it's lovely, of course, but the real satisfaction is internal.' 'So,' I say, 'you don't have to cast your bread upon the waters?' 'Of course one does, because one has become a member of that company of people who do, so it's nice to share it and get feedback and see a little bit how one is doing.

'Lionel [Abrahams] influenced my poetry writing tremendously because . . . you know when one falls in love with people – and I've fallen in love fairly regularly throughout my life – you always want to write a great poem about it, even if you throw it away. I suppose I didn't think of it [poetry] as a serious thing that I could do as well as the next person, until I joined Lionel's writing group at the Art Foundation. I never took it seriously, as something that I could do, before that. And then I found that when I was in that group, I did quite well, people responded quite well to what I wrote. And that was pretty soon after I met him. After I met him the first time, I went home and wrote a poem about him and I gave it to him. And he was quite tickled.'

ODE FOR FELIX

Ho ho! a friend!
I've found a friend
and what a friend is he!
With graceful beard and gentle eye
right merrily bent on me.

A mossy cardigan hangs round
his small and skinny bod;
an elf he seems
but what a bloke –
a huge enormous gorgeous bloke
a mighty magic spelling bloke –
a sort of ink-stained god.

With ginger pop and licorice
he weaves a crafty net.
An unsuspecting maiden I
all smitten in his web do lie:
'Dear Spider,' is my happy cry
'I'm jolly glad we met.'

'You've written several novels?'

'Yes I have. I've had two of them published. And three biographies. I was especially pleased with the first novel which was *The Killing Bottle* – part of my love affair with what was then known as the Eastern Transvaal and the whole escarpment scene there. We used to go there when I was married to my first husband. We panned for gold in the rivers; Pilgrims Rest, Sabie, Graskop, we had a wonderful time. You get these tiny little black speckles which you are told authoritatively, is gold. No, we didn't make a fortune. [That part of the world] is not so nice now. There were no tarred roads up there then, in the early 1960s, they were all sand roads. If you wanted to find God's Window, someone would tell you to look for a weird-shaped stone and a red tree beside the road, and that's where you had to turn off into the bush and go another mile or two before suddenly arriving at that stupendous view. It was completely unspoiled terrain; no advertisements, no car parks, no tour buses. I love wild South Africa – Prince Alfred's Pass, the Eastern Cape, the spring flowers of Namaqualand. But Mpumulanga remains my favourite place, although Sappi has done its best to cover it with pine trees.'

I once learned that Lionel and Jane read books to one another. I suggested that it was so beautifully old fashioned and asked Jane what it meant to them? They read literature, never a newspaper '[I hate newspapers']. 'We did it for the shared love of story. The significance of stories for me is that for as long as I can remember, when it actually began I have no idea, my father used to tell me a story every night. He made them up on the spur of the moment and it was always about the same set of characters: the Wicked Windy Witch who had a castle on Black Mountain and a dwarf as her servant who was hideous and totally stupid, and she had a dragon as a guard dog. I used to say, daddy make her do something really wicked this time. I couldn't get enough wickedness. Those stories went on for years and years. My father worked in the Bank of England and during the war the Bank was evacuated to the country and he only came back every other weekend. When he was away, no story, and this was the reason for teaching myself to read, because then I could still have my story.

'My father has remained the person about whom I say, what would Pa do in this situation? Both for me and for my brother he was the person admired above all other people. If I'm in any doubt over a moral issue I still say – 'what would Pa do?' Now that I think about it I had an incredibly safe childhood from an emotional point of view. I was in no doubt about what I was allowed and not allowed to do, there were quite definite boundaries. I had a mother who maybe was a little over . . . um . . . she was a little bit like an emotional tin opener, she always wanted to know what I was thinking and what I was feeling so I tended to shut up. Didn't tell her. But I had no doubt that I would be put first in any situation, my well-being was what mattered for her.'

I comment that Jane joined Lionel's writing group soon after meeting him and now some years after his death she's still running the group. 'Yes, it never stopped. After he died everybody said, please, let's go on. And it's a very valuable thing, it's a wonderful thing, actually. I had no formal academic training apart from a good English school, I didn't go to university. So fortunately, I remember very little about the theory – I do it by instinct or intuition. It's very liberating. There have been one or two people we've had through the workshop who kept on trotting out theories. Lionel used to shut them up like one o' clock because it really doesn't help, and so do I. And there are so many writing groups where in response to everything that comes up they say – oh, I love it, that's wonderful, lovely poetry! And I don't think that's helpful either. I try to be constructive in my criticism. Lionel's approach was, is this perfect that I'm hearing? And if not, how could it be made better? That was his approach, not what's wrong with it. We try to do the same thing. I'm also a student here, my stuff is listened to as well.' I suggest that the continuing group is almost a memorial to Lionel. 'Yes, in a way, although we've largely forgotten that. His portrait looks down [from above the fireplace] at us rather disapprovingly but I know he'd be glad that it was still going. The original group, which started around 1975, has changed of course, with one or two exceptions.'

I ask her to mention some of the group's writers who later became well known.

'There were quite a few. Lionel Murcott, E.M.Macphail, Zachariah Rapola, Joanne Fedler, Maureen Isaacson, David Medalie, Graeme Friedman... I don't really like mentioning names because there are probably many which should be mentioned that I've forgotten.

'I never encourage somebody to go on writing who I really think doesn't have it. I think there are all too many writers in the world who don't have it and who all the same get published and clutter the bookshops with second-rate stuff. I'm a terrible snob when it comes to creative writing. I only want to encourage the people with real talent. I once had the hideous experience of a radio interview. I can't remember who the interviewer was, but she said to me, do you think anyone can write? She was so clearly expecting the answer, yes. And I said, no, I don't think so. Practice is essential, but if you haven't got a certain talent in the first place, leave it alone. There's a sort of stream through history of wonderful stuff and I want to support that stream and not get bogged down in the dross.

'I do have one thought that might sound contrary to that, and it applies to any poem that has ever been written by anybody. Poems are the highest form of language that expresses what it is to be human. Good poems, bad poems, whatever, classical poems, lyric poems, sonnets, even slam poetry. All in some way or another express what it is to be human. Someone wanted to say something badly enough to put it into the best words they could. Therefore they are expressing, whether they know it or not, what it means to be their unique selves.'

Jane speaks about the 'Greats.'

'Well, I suppose the first name that springs to mind is Keats. And coming top of the list of poems is his Ode to a Grecian Urn. I was lucky to have a real enthusiast of Romantic Poetry as a teacher when I was sixteen, seventeen at school. I suddenly saw, click, what poetry could do, when I discovered Keats. And I can't not mention Shakespeare. Shakespeare was so much more than a poet that it's difficult to add him to a list confined to poetry. Again I was very, very lucky: I wasn't given Shakespeare to study in school before I'd seen several of the plays as a child. Shakespeare is not meant to be studied in school, you're meant to sit in the audience and then you can get enthusiastic. I suppose some of the great speeches in Shakespeare are still my favourite bits of poetry of all time. The Chorus in Henry V for example. I also love John Donne, Thomas Traherne, Yeats . . .'

I ask, 'Who are the locals whom you find stimulating?' 'Gus Ferguson,' she responds.

'He does with poetry what Herman Charles Bosman did with stories – he shows us to ourselves. With great humour and affection. Patrick Cullinan, Don McLennan, Douglas Livingstone. But it's the members of my own writing group that I find most stimulating: they really are an inspiration in all their different ways. I think we all feel lucky to have each other.' Among the Moderns, Eliot is not a favourite. 'I like the unique, the unusual. I enjoy poetry very much but it's the oddities. Stevie Smith is one of them. It's the unpredictable, the quirky, that I go for.'

I ask about life without Lionel. Jane, deeply sighing, and slowly gathering her words, 'I was tremendously helped by knowing that he died when he needed to. Life had just become too uncomfortable for him. He would have hated to be hospitalized (his kidneys had packed up), to be on dialysis. And he was working twenty-four hours before he died, which was so wonderful, and so what he would have asked for. If he could have chosen when and how to die that would have been it. That helped me tremendously, to know that and be quite sure about it. It helped me to let go. I was also helped to let go by being with him when he died and could help the process, come to terms with the process as it was happening. And to help him to go quickly, not to hang on and hang on, and everybody bustle around with the life support machines like they do in hospitals. He was in ICU, he'd been taken in the day before, but they left me alone with him. They didn't try to resuscitate. There was no drama; which was great, wonderful, for us both. I have a very strong personal conviction that I will be with him again at some stage. That also helped. Enormously.

'Even so, it was a very great shock, because, until an hour before he died, we had no idea that he was that bad. The night before, he was in the hospital and he'd been talking and laughing with his friends Hillary and Anne. When I left I said, bye, bye, I'll see you in the morning before I go to work. That was the situation when I left him the night before. And I went to sleep and I woke up the next morning to a phone call from the hospital to say, Mr Abrahams is not so good. Which I realized at once was a euphemism for 'Get here!' So I got there, how I drove there I have no idea, but I did. And he was still with us for about an hour after that, but I could see he was wanting to go, I could see he was trying.

'So all that was tremendously . . . I feel very blessed to have had that experience. It reconciled me to the whole idea of being without him in the physical. I'm sure he wrote that sonnet with me, quite sure, or anyway he was hovering there when I wrote it. And so I was enabled to come to terms with being on my own. I like my own company. I would never dream of sharing my life with anybody else. When you have had the perfect relationship, which it really was, I mean we were incredibly harmonious, we fitted each other so well. When you have had a perfect relationship you don't want to follow it with a second best. So life without Lionel is different but also very full. Because not having him any more, I could take up stuff which I really didn't feel I wanted to leave him for while he was still here. For example, the

Johannesburg Bach Choir. Joining that more or less pulled my threads together after he died. Having something really beautiful to do and be involved in – it was great healing [softly and reflectively] ja . . . ja.'

I tipped Jane into rounding off the interview. 'When somebody says that, one immediately becomes totally tongue-tied. Well, only to say that it is the greatest, greatest satisfaction in the world to write something and work on it for x number of days or weeks and then look at it and say, 'I've got it!' I have actually expressed what I want to express in the way I want to express it. If I get goose bumps, then I know it's finished. That would be my round off.'

□

This was written after I sang with the Johannesburg Bach Choir as part of a special service at the German Lutheran Church in Bryanston.

BACH IN WINTER

The Thomaskirche – icy cold:
the choir sits haloed in their breath
the strings knuckle their hands
turn up the corners of their scores
and wait, tapping their bows.
The congregation, hatted and shawled
shuffle their way forward
thread themselves along the pews
the oboist
feeling his coming notes with the fingers of his mind
holds his oboe under his jacket
warming it against his heart.
The gentle harpsichord
stands in the midst, a poem in pale wood
its carved keys waiting to weave
the melody. And then they come
the bishop in green, the pastor in white
treading cheerfully amongst their flock.
The conductor collects eyes
raises his baton
and Johann Sebastian blesses the air.

□

The first line is a salute to Catullus (Roman poet 84-54 BC), one of the most poignant writers of love (and hate) poetry in history.

HOMAGE TO CATULLUS

White white day in the calendar
even though it was a rainy night.
On a rainy night he suddenly
pulled me into his warmth
licensed me
      to take the blind woman's way
      to discover by touch his sweetness
          to understand
          what must be forgone
          what distilled:
the essence of love which transcends years.

☐

MICROLOVE

If I rake with my tiny nails
the shining furrows in your hair
comb your eyelashes as you sleep
if I put my nose into your ear
and puff my small breaths into your head
will pictures of me start playing
in the movies of your mind?

When you notice me
I leap and run
over and under and in between
your body my playgound.

But I want to taste your birthday
and I wish I could get to see what you look like inside.
I am the mouse in your pocket
and my world turns
to the strong beautiful beat of your heart.

Frank Meintjies

I meet Frank, career journalist and columnist, lifelong poet, at his place of work, the Nelson Mandela Centre of Memory in Houghton. His major but not the only task there, is to coordinate and manage the information around the annual Nelson Mandela Day. He collects me in the reception area with its stunning, broad banded carpet and statues of the great man, and we walk to a conference area with excellent acoustics. We know each other vaguely, having read at the same festival, a year ago. I tell him a little about myself, later realizing that we were on opposite sides during the dramatic days when black trade unions were first legally recognized. I outline my reasons for conducting conversations with poets.

Then we get down to business and I ask Frank, 'How did you get involved in poetry?'

'My involvement started in schooldays through an English teacher. He taught us very, very well. He gave us creative exercises, plenty of writing exercises, and I decided to branch into poetry. Most of the creative activities he gave the class were prose. But then he also showed and shared with us some of his own poetry – and I think that was the spark. That was around 1974.'

'So the spark was a creative teacher?'

'Yes, he drew us into literature in quite a powerful way, made the prescribed texts real to us and allowed us to see how some of them can have current meaning and apply in our lives. And he overlaid these with his own writing which he shared with us. The teacher originally came from Bechet College in Durban and was posted over to Pietermaritzburg to our community school.'

'Would you say that was a fortunate accident?'

'Yes, I think it was, it seemed to set me on a path . . . by the way I cannot recall any other person in the same cohort who also embarked on a path of writing. Then I went off to university and, even though I did not initially enroll in the arts, I maintained a sense of working with writing and with poetry. That move to the University of the Western Cape (UWC) was a good move because it was the area in which people were using poetry in a whole lot of different ways, including people like Adam Small, Hein Willemse, Howard Gabriel and James Matthews. I was also exposed to black consciousness writers who were talking of Afrikaans for liberation and concepts such as black English. Breyten Breytenbach and his writing had a strong influence among the Afrikaans speaking poets on the campus. There were some notable poets and writers who I met during my first few months. They were all on campus: Hein Willemse, Andries Oliphant, Gerhard Botha and Ronnie Swartz. They wrote prolifically and found ways to distribute their writing on campus. And much of the writing was influenced by the kind of 'ways of seeing' that Breytenbach was noted for. The writing was strident, very outspoken, but it was also very non-realist writing, with striking imagery and which also, in many cases, pushed aside the conventions of language. Translating that into English wasn't easy; however, with my own writing, I operated in a parallel stream, trying to find my way, trying to find my feet. My writing wasn't particularly good at the time, but I continued with the work.'

'You found yourself there at UWC in a political hotbed, is that right?'

'Yes, this is what informed much of the writing there; it was a political hotbed and there was room for involvement in student politics. By the end of my first year I was elected into a position at the residences and together with others I continued the tradition of using the residences as a place to hold cultural activities and events. We ran a magazine edited by Hein Willemse, called *Megafoon*, [Megaphone]. At the same time I was involved in several clubs, we ran regular film showings, partly for income generation, but the films were very carefully selected for being sympathetic to people's political ideals, and to self expression and affirmation. So we chose many films with black characters. Sydney Poitier movies, for example, were quite prominent in those days. Then there was a movie such as *Black Like Me*, in which a white characters darkened his skin and experienced what it meant to be black.'

Here we spend a moment or two reminiscing about Poitier's famous film, *Guess Who's Coming to Dinner*, about a young white woman who takes her black fiancé into the parental home for the first time.

Frank continues, 'So the thing about political hotbeds is that it's fine to mobilize large numbers of students to move in a huge mass from the administration block to the gate to protest there, and to make the university dysfunctional. But it's also as important to have an underlay of cultural activities which inform and educate. And which allow and prepare students to form arguments about what the current reality is and what the alternative reality should be. And for us on the creative side, it is much better if such arguments are formulated creatively. You're speaking about human existence and you want to move away from the didactic, from sloganeering. There's always a tension . . .' I interrupt to suggest that it's a moving away from ideological clichés. 'Yes,' says Frank, 'because while those are useful, they have their limits, they reach their dead ends. Sometimes we operated in parallel with those clichés so that in the same political meeting there would be a request for some artistic presentation so that one deepens the understanding of why people become involved [in politics].' I suggest that Frank had a sophisticated perception of his political role at a young age. He replies, 'Yes and no. All this was new to me; at the same time, my understanding was growing. We were having debates about whether social change was going to be the mirror image of the situation then – a reversal where black domination replaces white domination – or would there be a complete transformation. We were also looking to black theology and were involved in a Christian club which was affiliated to an organization headed by Dr Alan Boesak. He was articulate, writing about theology and human existence and how it should express itself in conditions of oppression and slavery. So we were thinking quite deeply.'

I ask Frank whether he was writing much poetry at the time. 'I was writing a lot of poetry though it wasn't very good! I was submitting to the *Megaphone*. It was a magazine full of art work, striking drawings and prints from artists like Andries Oliphant.'

What about early, home, literary influences? 'No we didn't have a wide range of books in the home although there were some books. I was one of eight siblings, one sister and the rest brothers. My brothers were mostly older than me. One read James Hadley Chase [popular and somewhat lurid US crime writer at the time] and another subscribed to *Readers' Digest* and was sent *Readers' Digest* condensed books. There were also other action-orientated paperbacks and westerns around the house. This is not the kind of material I would read now but they were there and the condensed books provided a lot of easy and pleasant material. And I guess at a certain age, easier reading is a lot better and, though I haven't thought about it much, I think I read many books at that time.'

I ask about stimulation from the brothers.

'To an extent . . . most of my brothers didn't advance far beyond standard eight. One of them actually dropped out after standard six; that brother, Jimmy, had played a key role. He was thinking about political ideas and black consciousness. He was a friend of (Black Consciousness leader) Henry Isaacs (who was associated with Steve Biko and was part of the BC movement). Isaacs was under house arrest some three streets away. My brother and friends would visit and they'd come back and talk among themselves, not with me, because I was much younger, but I'd overhear the conversation. So I was eavesdropping on this brother, and I always saw him and the others reading even if it was Chase or westerns. But I had no children's books. It was only at school that I was introduced to Shakespeare and poetry. We did Hamlet as our school play. We were immersed in our prescribed books and with the help of our teacher we were very active participants, sometimes enacting parts. And we also had – in grades ten, eleven and twelve – prescribed books of collected essays and books like *The Old Man and the Sea* and *The Snow Goose* and *The Small Miracle*. And we lapped them up because these were works of greater substance, books that we would never get at home. Also, I started using the library.'

I now turn to Frank's poetry. 'Is my perception that there is a great deal of anger in your work, correct?'

'I would like my poems to be edgy and I think there's a great deal of pain in the world. Of course, people can write in other ways and all the other ways are valid. However, I would like a good number of my poems to reflect the tension in society and that pain. I always joke when I speak to young people interested in my poetry, and say, "The first poem in any collection of mine will always contain the word blood." 'I come out of that school in which the likes of Breytenbach and Wopko Jensma, artists such as Fikile and Sedumedi, as well as black feminist poets such as Bell Hooks, had great influence. They really wanted to shake people up – shock them a bit, get them out of their comfort zone. But my poems are much more balanced now.'

'Why more balanced now when we live in such dreadful political times?'

'More balanced in that I have changed and am more willing to consider that the half-empty cup is also half full. And I'm able to appreciate – much more now – the fact that people do have relationships, go on with their lives and pursue certain personal goals, despite oppression. That there is so much in life that is positive – so much of value that people and communities extract from the world around them.

Even in poor communities, there is life and vibrancy. For your own reasons, you may want to paint things in a one sided light . . . but on any given day, there'd be a wedding, some would be relaxing after work, the vehicles would be hooting, and people would be spending on the bridesmaids dresses . . . and so life goes on.

'And I think, the appreciation of a flower is a firm response to all the hardship. It's a counterbalance. As a friend puts it, everyone has a right to beauty. An artist must also make beautiful things. So when you're crafting poems and stories, if it's just angry and there's nothing creative and dynamic about it, it's not good enough; it doesn't pass muster. On the other hand, if you fashion your words well & pay attention to your craft, anyone with a love of words would read it; whether they agree with your sentiments or not, they may be entranced and seduced. And part of liberation, not just political liberation but broader liberation, relates to being able to appreciate beauty, to play with the material that's available and to make one's own beauty. Any denial that we appreciate things that are well-crafted, and an insistence that that there's only an angry mode, often adds to the problem. So I've been through a journey that has led to growth and greater depth. I think many people don't understand it, this interplay between anger and beauty, even to this day.

'So for example when you speak of poor people, who are we talking about? And to assume that someone with poverty of the stomach also always suffers the other poverties, is making a serious mistake. So there are all kinds of poverty and, once you get to this kind of depth, you see that solutions are often embedded in the 'problem' you want to take on. You see that instead of appealing for outside solutions, you work with what is available in communities, you work with what is beautiful, their aesthetic, what appeals and energizes, and you bring that out as a celebration. If we can bring more sound, more rhythm, more of that popular vibrancy into our poetry, our poetry will be much more powerful. If you think of it as the beauty of pain and the stress within joy, all are there, and try to capture it all.'

'How,' I ask Frank, 'does a poem come to you?'

'There are two ways. One is the flash, the moment when you are on your own, and when the image and the clear sense of a poem comes to you.'

'What do you do with the flash?'

'If I have my note book, I'm able to write that down. And if I don't write it down, I am sometimes able to recall it hours or days later. At other times, it will be gone. I estimate that I lose more than fifty percent of such nascent poems. In my latest book, I have a poem called *Leaf*. It's about a leaf that remains stubbornly green in a brown bush. And the poem states that this leaf didn't get the message that a change of seasons has taken place. The poem was included (in the collection) almost exactly as it was first written.

'So that's the one way and then the other way: I start off with a feeling about something and a desire to write a poem about it. A few words come to me and I begin to associate them with that feeling and it plays on my mind for two or three days. Let's take an example: I think about my late father, and I think about the mixture of feelings I have towards him – the love, the kind of support and guidance I got, but also the areas in which he came short, such as the aversion to speaking about feelings and emotions. I will carry the feeling for several days and think:

here is a possible poem. In my mind it will be a poem called "Father". And then I will sit down and craft it but wait maybe another two or three more days for all the dimensions of that poem to become clearer. Following this, I may add a few stanzas much later. Compare this to *Leaf* which I penned in one go.

'Still talking about a fictional 'Father' poem, memory is significant; memory at a personal, community or country level. Memory is always charged, it contains contradictions, it is often more complicated than we realize. Once one really starts to work with memory you begin to see how selective one's own memory is and how memory of the same event differs for different people. And some memories even differ from the record. The sense one has of the sequence, how things happened, takes a certain form in my mind. Yet when I look at the actual record, I find that my sequence is all wrong. So you have to do a great deal of checking: was this 1967 or 1968? Which event happened first? As such, memory is selective and we ourselves select. And memory in South Africa is a major issue. In a sense we are still at war with each other: what happened, who was there, what was the impact, whose memories are more important, what part of memory should be affirmed, which should be downplayed? And there are some people who say get over it, move on, and there are others who say we can't move on until we've dealt with it a bit more. The Truth Commission took the view that before we move on, we need to have the facts and the truth on the table.'

'How many books of poetry have you published?'

'My main outlet has been anthologies and journals. But I've just brought out, this month, my second book. My first was called *My Rainbow* and the current one is titled *Connexions*.'

'Do you believe you've been recognized as a poet?'

'That's a very good point to discuss. I don't believe there's much open discussion about this. I don't think I'm a very recognized poet; I don't think I could just send my poetry to a publisher and just expect them to publish it. So both my books have been self-published and I think they 'hold'. Obviously I try to do what I imagine a publisher would do: I try to sift out and exclude those poems which I think are not good enough or which won't be good quality for readers. Before finalizing the collection, I ask third parties to identify four or five poems which they think should not be included. Then, after publication, when I give friends or associates one of my books, I tell them I want some feedback. All they need to do is tell me which poems they really liked. It's very interesting. I get a lot of surprises. The poems I consider to be weaker are often greatly enjoyed by such reviewers. I am therefore convinced that the selections in my collections are justified. However, I still have that sense of uncertainty about the poems I chose to exclude (at the earliest stages) from the draft manuscript; I reread them and wonder why I left them out. I then use some of them at public readings because sometimes an excellent poem in a book just falls flat in a reading environment; especially with a voice like mine, which isn't very loud.

'I like to participate in poetry readings. They bring one out of one's isolation and into a public space and – if one is lucky – one gets that engagement, especially if the group is smaller. So that's the cup half-full side. And then the cup half-empty side is that many poets and rappers invest in performance – and that investment in performance gives audiences experience and expectation of these readings that I can't live up to. So at all readings, I always ask the Master of Ceremonies to go first. Because then I can get mine done, relax and enjoy the rest of it. But also because there are often poets who are skilful performers coming after my reading, and then I don't have to live up to them. Although I enjoy most of performance poetry, as a poet I don't function well in the performance space. This is because the audiences develop these set expectations of what a poem is and what it should do. I find that when I take part in public poetry readings, if I go first, members of the audience listen better because they have not yet been attuned to the "expert" performers. In the case of many black female poets, it's performance as much as the words that has impact and has created such a big following for them. Using the performance platform, poetry is a drama that they enact; they bring a unique power and life to the work even in those instances where the poem, were it printed on a page, would be weak or insipid. But they enliven it through the dramatization; so the combination makes quite a powerful statement. But for the artist who is primarily a performance poet, there could be challenges when bringing his or her work out in print. An idea might be to have your writing tightened up for the page. A good editor could help to take out certain things which work as aids in the performance but are superfluous or dilute the impact on the page. Generally, many, many young people think of themselves as rappers or rapper-poets. There's a huge movement out there and it's positive. They're a dynamic force; poetry is so alive and young people are keeping it alive.

'I do, in my writing, talk quite a lot about the process of poetry, the process of writing the poem. In my current collection, in a piece entitled *How to Trim a Poem*, I deal with what is involved in shaping a poem and the process of editing. Many of the more outspoken black and white Afrikaans poets I encountered in the early days, because many of them were outcasts, were edgy, rebellious and dispensed with language and grammar formalities. Quite a few of them were actually artists as well, sometimes abstract and surreal, and they brought that sense into poetry. Then there is the influence of the well-known black poets who have that innate ability to create images and metaphor, who know how to work with the symbolic and to mix different traditions. These poets worked with language in bold, powerful and sometimes brash ways, fearlessly articulating what the community sees, what they observe and the feelings of their time.

'But there's writing beyond poetry which is also important. For instance, a writer like James Baldwin or the work of Bell Hooks, the way they were using language to communicate deep responses to society and their place within it. Take the writing of someone like Richard Rive. I don't write prose but you could see how he, writing about District Six and the removals, uses characters, and through a story conveys something deep about that human experience. Take the strident voice of James Baldwin and the public and personal issues that he's grappling with and note how he brings those into his writing – there's a great deal to learn from that. And then, of course, the influence of the English and American writers, people like Sylvia Plath. There you get content that is psychological, but communicated in a way that rises above the self-indulgent and is a comment on society.'

We talk about the cultural environment and support for artists. Frank maintains, 'South Africa faces a major problem in the cultural arena. We lack sufficient spaces where people from diverse backgrounds and different walks of life can interact meaningfully. Which is why the Melville Poetry Festival is so remarkable, one of those rare cases where you have poets from different backgrounds as well as different generations getting together to celebrate poetry – a festival of pleasure in and a celebration of the Word and how it functions in the world.

'And then, there is the big problem of the publishing arena: manuscripts from new writers, many of them publishable works, are piling up but publishers don't see a big enough market for poetry. Ironically, this type of blockage in the system can sometimes be useful because it tends to ensure that what comes through is the best. At the same time – and this is what we have now – things can become too constricted. It means that many, many voices which should be heard are being excluded, including poets that write in languages other than English. So the average publisher tells you from the outset that they're not interested in poetry. Because we are in a commercial and capitalist environment, and publishing houses seek a substantial return, we need a system which allows for the subsidization of publishers. Without subsidies poetry will continue to suffer; the wealthy can publish their own works but working class and community poets will be disadvantaged. The Lotto used to play a useful role in providing small publishers with some resources to bring out journals, anthologies or single-author publications. But, from what I know, they have become unreliable and inconsistent in terms of their support. We also do need more channels where writers can be afforded time (to write) on a paid basis. I'm not sure about the schemes for that, but there should be certain awards which would allow active writers to spend six months or so devoted to their writing. So we need private institutions and public institutions to make facilities available for writers. Without such support systems you won't have an optimal diversity of literary voices.'

'How do you see the academic influence on poetry?'

'Attention begins with reviews, and few book review sections in the newspapers take poetry seriously. Even if they are pressed for space they could devote a small percentage of column inches to write sensibly about poetry books, but they don't bother. And when you escalate that to the academic level, the marginalization of local poetry is reproduced. And so we get an undervaluing of things that are important. We locate ourselves within and appreciate world literature, but we need to pay greater attention to our own literature. Local poetry is a complete Cinderella. But poetry is a very genuine art form – so many poets continue to write, expecting nothing in return, producing despite a largely unsupportive environment.

'Having said this, I would like to pay tribute to the kind of champions that have been there in the poetry world. And these champions I would define as people who themselves obviously write poetry but who have an added dimension – they are active as organizers of spaces and platforms. On both sides – in the black community and in white community – you find such activists. Alongside their creative work they work tirelessly to creating avenues for others. Some of them have brought out their own journals, often out of their own pockets.

'If you look at the Melville Poetry Festival and events like the Franschoek Literary Festival – which reaches a more confined audience but enriches the arts more broadly – one sees that there are people on all sides of the spectrum who step forward to create spaces and platforms. Others undertake non-profit publishing open to all writers. Botsotso, Timbila and wRite Associates are good examples. And then there's another level where some organizations like Botsotso are lobbying policy makers about certain changes relating to the book publishing industry and the purchasing policy of libraries. One needs to salute such poetry activists, because such activism is sometimes a tradeoff: do you spend time organizing or do you focus on your creative work? We have to honour those people. They are real 'troopers', the old war horses such as Gus Ferguson, Vonani Bila, Myesha Jenkins and Allan Horwitz, not forgetting the work and contribution of the late Lionel Abrahams, and the kind of nurturing and inspirational work that he has done. Such persons have continued year in and year out, unsung and with very little support from other sources. They have greatly enriched literature in South Africa.'

□

My brother Michael died of cancer. He was a big, broad-shouldered man. He had worked as a handyman, laid bricks, poured cement and did bits of carpentry. He also baked cakes, large ones, and at Christmas time took orders from paying customers. Michael had a bright aura that leavened family gatherings. With the exception of the last weeks of his life, his booming voice, great laugh and humour carried him through the ups and downs of life. Whenever I read this poem, I relive the pain of I felt on seeing his wonderful personality changed under the distortion that cancer brought.

michael

from a brown bottle
i poured the morphine
into a spoon

my brother lies on the bed
smallness
taken over his frame

stalled, arrested, stymied
- the mighty project
that was a life

a colour-coded thread, spanning
fads, seasons, old & new exclusions, phases of songs, isms
hairstyles weird & wonderful; wounds
& a country stepping forth from wombs of oppression

by the bedside
in early days
teasing remarks
fall like flakes in the room
light talk, in-jokes, the
quips about the minor dramas of a plain household
those early days …
but now, i feel
a tautness of jaw & face

(as if breathing itself
rubs salt into
lesions of cells)
pointing to a drawer
michael said, get my will,
let's check
he wants to make sure
the papers are in order

in the end, all come to rest
the big laugh, that consummate smile
the cake-bakes, the cement-laying hands
the work with screwdrivers & drills
at varsity residences
even the fingers
that once played the shakers for the lollies

the brutal invasion
of tranquillity

in the universe (of this room)
a stillness
your body rotating around your soul
a quiet equilibrium
a descending reverence

weeping postponed
at this moment, not even
the small comfort of tears

☐

Written in the months following the death of Whitney Houston, this poem is about the effect of her music in working class communities. Young women in such communities find their own voices using Whitney's songs. This can often be seen on the stages of music reality shows where girls from humble backgrounds display zest, talent and a moment of self-actualisation while singing one of her chart-toppers.

voice

voice sinewy, voice bird-skin tough
voice that journeys
& turns
& pirouettes
on boardwalks

in the lane, between the flats
in the location
or in the flattest Cape
present, in the thirteen-year-old
that sings herself beyond her limits
beyond uneven fences
beyond the wasteland

whitney, roaming the land
one foot in a hotel bath
another on a stage
a smile, breaking through the make-up
another day
dawns
best-friend real

voice elongates
flexes
as it wanders
the cosmos fields
down lanes
over streams
between the homesteads
voice that burns the fields, orange flames

in the gorges
between high buildings
at the all-night shop
at the troyeville garage
by the alex hairdresser

& the internet shop with its old computers
beyond the bars
beyond the soullessness
in nights of elegance
voice canters on, covers ground
rises
whirls & wheels
dips back
to caress
the grubby streets

☐

A conversation about fruit, an appreciation of fruit – where it comes from and the distance it has travelled to the bowl on my table. On reading the poem, my daughter told me: "I have only once had an apple which still had a leaf attached to it."

golden delicious

the supermarket
stashes
the decanted apple boxes
in the grimy alley

from ceres, from elgin, from tzaneen

in the storefront
the apples, neatly lined in trays
four rand each, the shelf tag says
under fluorescent lights

on a shelf across the aisle
tightly swaddled in plastic
punnets of six
light green, shiny red or
toffee-apple green

i bite into the sweetness
tear a piece from the whole
small secretions of foam
enjoyment, written in teethmarks

far away on distant erfs,
the farm, the tree, the morning spider, the apple-picker
beyond range
no line of sight
in the shop
i want to see apple boxes, scuffed from journey
touch the cardboard,
the polystyrene trays, the odd leaf
see name of farm & region

sweeter still are
apples that stay true to who they are
under
tubes of lights

somewhere: original grit
the valley's slope
worker's sweat
prickles of translucent dew
long before the polishing

near the door, a fat man in a red suit
rings a bell
walking with my ten year old
she wants to know
why i say
apples shouldn't be golden

☐

*Small towns are distinctive. Unlike the small towns in the Karoo, the ones on South
Africa's east coast are English speaking. The poem does not refer to a specific place but
it does draw on the experience of a friend, a woman priest, who was posted to such a
town. She faced years of uphill – conservative congregants who squirmed at sermons on
social justice and macho board members who continuously reminded her that it was
their church.*

seaside town

south of durban
the small seaside town
lies cosy & curled
wedged between canefield acres & the sea
big waves & rocks
- it lies sedate in the off-season sun

quaint shopping centre, doctor, dentist, a second-hand bookshop or two
vet, video store, pizza den
friendly service & bucolic pleasantries for village people

gardeners, domestic workers, labourers, galley hands at the b&b, pool cleaners,
fixers, street sweepers
there – but not there
life is over the hill, some 12 kilometres away

especially in off-season
eyes of the neighbourhood watch
peer
strangers who look like the residents
always welcome, cosseted
& other strangers: a beady eye

peaceful now, shielded
from the breakers that are South Africa
land claims, far off rumours, strikes, tsunamis on faraway beaches
    only small violations, the breaking of window panes,
    disturb the night's rest

two years ago
my friend marina was exiled there
she heads the school
tries to be true, tries to be real
but how can you wear your style

speak your truths here, in this space
no poems, no provocative plays, no dreadlocked troubadours, no pink
                                                    parades
no 'red ants' down the road, dislodging land invaders

they tell you
this place is special

they have a way of doing things
that's how it's always been
the residents embrace the new locals
retired executives from the mines
they bring in money, they bring stubborn strength
they remind you: it's their school, not yours
it's a white town, marina tells me
workers trek in daily from over a hill
living their parallel lives
their settlements a dam
water trickling into the nearby hamlets

old in the new
refuge from the wind
a calm inlet
small place tucked between main road & the sea

i hate & like the place
with its ice cream cones
the chipstix van with serving hatch
the sandy bodies & the beachside showers
the small lodges
offering a room & hot breakfast for the middle class
the ag pleez daddy song, so hauntingly familiar

□

*A key assertion in this poem is the circular argument: we as poets write simply
because we write. Anything and anything can provide an excuse to write. It also
argues that we are moved to put pen to paper because we are alive, because we observe
and because we, even in small ways, enter into the experiences of others. This poem
explores personal reasons for writing poetry. At the same time, I recall that when I was
writing it, I consciously wanted a strong reference to "we" throughout the poem. The
"we" conveys my connection to other poets, ones I meet at informal readings, Botsotso
activities and other cultural events.*

we write what we like

(apologies to biko)

we write what we like
because
when some of us die
or disappear, like jensma
who will find the body?
who will stalk the grains of truth?
will the ones to come
find the spoor?

we write what we like
because when the black bird
stands over the child
poised for its entrails
the earth has died
as much
as if hit
by a thermonuclear wave

we write as we like, because
of the millions
who were loaded into holds, some decanted
into landfills, others dying
water-deaths
   listen! the sighs
   ride the seas
   the bones call out through our pens

we write as we like
because smoke was rising, grey columns
cigar smoke, when the generals
peered down
as crowds ran
first in, then out, of stadiums
where the gunshots ring

we write what we like, also
because love (like anger
or, with the force of anger)
breaks through
cracks
in the old buildings

& small weeds squeeze forth
between
pavement slabs
where the bad boys
once fought

& because
the rows of little houses
sprout patterns & braided heads & vendor-stalls & rap songs & graffiti
& because curry smells
brew & ripen
as the day unravels

our pens won't self-muzzle or stay put
because at tonkwane, in magaliesburg
the immense gorges gape
& the kranse
scratch at the sky, the itching
causing storms

unconsoled
(our pens weep) because
as the blesbok's shin
caught in the trap
leaks blood
the calf must move on
in search of the brook

we write
words we choose, words that choose us
words that lasso & grip us
because ... under a tree
children read a book
& the story flits
from branch to branch
from artery to artery
& back to protruding roots
of the gnarled tree

we write what we like
since
on fridays, (even in darker times, days of tanks & curfews
when bullets punched holes in school uniforms)
the taxis hoot
coolly clustering

in the clutter of downtown life
waiting, lurking ... for the homeward push; salesmen call
& brenda's voice spits & steams
from giant speakers
& the next day
the wedding convoy slithers
to the city gardens, where
cameras click & pleasure bubbles forth
from stiff suits
& tight dresses

i spade words, spoon commas, similes & metaphors;
like a tube, i excrete
pastes of hard or soft colours;
blue green yellow black purple orange mustard
in ranging texts, filled with widows & orphans or peppered
with spaces that count as full stops
in lines that huddle
by cramped margins
i play
close to the edge
... i write what i like

Phillippa Yaa de Villiers

Phillippa is brown but she talks like a well educated, northern suburbs, white woman. Where do these social and racial contrasts come from? As a black child with loving white parents who were in denial of her true identity, she wrestled in our obsessive colour arena for all her early and contradictory life. While I sit horrified, she tells her heart rending and so South African story, in measured, unemotional and sometimes ironic tones, suggesting that at the age of 47, she's worked through and come to terms with much of the madness and the pain.

She tells me, 'After I was born in Hillbrow to an Australian woman, I was given up for adoption in 1966 and placed in the Princess Alice Adoption Home in Westcliff. I only found this out in 1998 when I got hold of my Child Welfare file and was able to discover the details of what had happened. This was because my parents (I'm speaking here of the people who brought me up) didn't tell me I was adopted until I was twenty. What I discovered from the Child Welfare file was that on the third day of her stay in hospital, my mother signed me off to the adoption home. The nurses were concerned because I had curly hair and thick lips. They accepted me but wanted to find out more about my father. My mother had put his name on the birth certificate; his name was Amamoo. That made them think: *there's something wrong here.*'

The adoption officials pursued various possibilities: Greek, Lebanese, Arab, Australian Aboriginal father were considered. Professor Phillip Tobias [geneticist/ anthropologist] and his colleague, Dr. de Villiers, were called in to study the child. They watched slides of Aboriginals and they tested me in various ways and they decided there was definitely reason to be suspicious. So the Home decided they couldn't give me up for adoption to a B+ or middle class home and that I would have to go to a to go to a working class home. And then months went by, nothing was happening and I was just getting bigger and less cute [laughter].

'So the Princess Alice Matron went back to Professor Tobias and asked him what should she do. And he said, *well, I'm not really into children* [laughter]. Then she walked past my adoptive mother's [Dr de Villiers] office. My mother said, *what are you doing with that baby, why is she here?* Matron explained. My mother said, *oh, it's that baby?* And she went home and spoke to her husband and her sons [who were grown up already] and they decided to adopt me. I moved into their Halfway House [Midrand] home on the day Hendrik Verwoerd was assassinated. And my parents decided that no one would tell me I was adopted.

'My adoptive mother is Dr Hertha de Villiers, a physical anthropologist and an anatomist. She taught at Wits in the Anatomy Dept. at Medical School and then she moved to the dental school. I'm supposed to be named after Prof. Tobias. My adoptive father was a working man, an artisan, not educated. He was proudly English speaking, but white working class, complete white working class.'

We come to Phillippa's schooldays.

'I started off at Assumption Convent, Maryvale. It was the first time I started interacting with people. It was complicated. I didn't enjoy it, I hated school. It was not good for me. My parents knew me as an outgoing child who got on with everybody. I just became very withdrawn at Assumption Convent. I grew up as an atheist so I didn't relate to the religion at all. And also no one could relate to me although there were other people who had very curly hair and dark skins – Portuguese girls – in all of the schools that I went to. I wondered about them. And I wondered whether other people wondered about me. And there were incidents – my first day at school I got thrown off the bus. When I was about eight, I was thrown out of the movies. My mother absolutely stuck by her conviction that I was white. She was completely in denial about what was happening.

'When I left home, I just wanted to get as far away as I could from Halfway House. White kids were saying things about black people and I just had to fit in because I was brought up there. I never felt as if I was really part of it. I just acted the part of Vice Head Girl at Waverly. A teacher contacted me on Facebook to say, *you were such a wonderful person . . . and I just can't believe . . .* Of course, now everyone knows that I'm not white. And I know as well. But then, everyone just really wondered, but no one could say anything because my mother was right there with the story. And my father just went along with it. They completely denied my reality.

'My mother loved one poem. She loved Cecil Day Lewis. She had a book of his poetry in the car and she would always recite this poem: *Is it far to go? A step, no further.* She was away a lot, she traveled, so I was left with my father looking after me. I learnt to read at the age of three. My father loved reading, he read compulsively. He struggled with his eyesight, he read those large print books He loved cowboy books and skop, skiet en donner. I used to lie with my head on his shoulder and read with him, I'd just look at the words and one day I just knew what they said. I don't know how it happened.'

I share with Phillippa, 'That's how I learnt to read at a similar age.'

'Reading was something my father and I did together. I grew up with Louis L'Amour and James Hadley Chase, Hammond Innes and Harold Robbins. And it was such an occasion when my mother went away. My father loved my mother but he was quite laid back. She was hard on herself and hard on those around her. I had a very close relationship with dad. When my mother went away we'd dress up to go to the airport, my father in his Safari Suit and me in anything my mother didn't want me to wear. In those days, to see someone off, was an occasion. And then my father and I would go to *Mr Prawn* in Savoy and have a 'slap up' meal and then one day my dad decided, *I'm signing you up for the library*. I was about six. Suddenly I had Enid Blyton and it was so boring after the blood and guts. And we'd go to the drive-in – totally forbidden when my mother was around. I had this secret life with my father, full of pleasures. We'd go to the drive-in and if it was age restricted we'd put a blanket over my head.' [This section is accompanied by much laughter]

I ask Phillippa how she came to poetry.

'I think as a little girl, I loved to play. I made things all the time. I would walk and conjure things from ordinary objects. I didn't have toys, my parents didn't do toys. Occasionally friends or relatives would give me one but I didn't know what to do with it or how to look after them, so they became ruined very quickly. I'd play with natural things. I once did a workshop on children's theatre with a Swedish director, and she asked, when was your first experience of beauty? I remembered this one time, I must have been about five, it was sunset, I watched the sun going down; the sunset was kind of greenish, you know when you see a slightly green sunset and there were Flying Ants and there'd been a storm and these Flying Ants were just flying up. My eyes filled with tears and I remember thinking, *am I sad?* And I realized I wasn't sad, I was crying because it was beautiful. This director said that that moment, when you first perceive beauty, is when you become an artist. She really affirmed me, because she told me this thing, she helped me to remember.

'I learnt to swim the same way I learnt to read. There was a pool at the house and my parents were terrified that something might happen. So before I could even properly walk, they threw me in the pool. So I always knew how to swim. I spent a lot of time there. And as I grew into school, the words started to come . . . with all the silence about my identity . . . I started writing and I wrote in a diary and I'd write my secret thoughts and I'd write secret letters to various people, imaginary people. I was very interested in historical characters. And I wrote to the characters in the skop, skiet and donners. I loved Tracey Dark. I was completely into her. I wanted to be her, to be psychic. And then I just started writing poems and I'd read them to my father. I really went underground when I was about twelve. I wrote a poem about fire, which was published in *The Star* newspaper but my teacher said that my mother had written it, that I hadn't written it. I completely stopped believing in myself which was the worst possible thing. She said, *you didn't write this!* in front of the whole class. Then I stopped showing anyone what I was writing. I stopped writing completely for a decade. I only wrote letters to people, post cards, little bits and pieces.'

At the age of twenty, Phillippa's life became particularly unsettled. She did little studying for her BA in Journalism at Rhodes. She became involved in 'smoking' and student politics and not only was she told then by her parents that she was adopted, but they also disowned her, largely for her radical anti-apartheid talk.

'Because I was involved in politics, my parents were scared. My mother just decided, *that's it!* My father came and told me I was adopted because they got a call from the Security Branch. I had a tantrum, it was very heavy. I said, *no I don't want to see you any more.* I felt completely abandoned. But my father always kept in contact, writing to me in his beautiful copper plate handwriting. Janet Heard, my best friend at the time, her family took me in. They became my family. And my friend Steven Markovitz.

'I completed university with a friend, Elaine Williams, who had a trust fund that stood surety for a bank loan. I had no idea of what I was going to do. I came to Jo'burg and once again this question of race popped up. Here's this person with a white accent, a white voice, thoroughly Western, phoning for job interviews. You get to the interview and, *sorry, we don't have work for you, sorry, the job's been filled.* My parents were no help. I just said, *I've got to get out of this country!*

'In 1988 I went to the United States. I couldn't get a job but I was working on a movie and I got a sugar daddy who paid my ticket to Los Angeles. At the time you weren't allowed to take money out of the country so you could make commission by taking money out for other people. I used that money to pay off my bank loan.'

Phillippa's experiences came apace. She dumped her sugar daddy and made new friends, moved into an apartment with a musician and a young studio executive, was taken in by a couple, not much older, who fussed over her. She waitressed and worked as a journalist and worked on a film with Danny Glover, *To Sleep with Anger*. US Blacks were fascinated by this representative African ['the real thing'] who quoted Shakespeare.

'It was all very liberating, but I was on my way somewhere. I had to find out who I was. I knew it was a creative thing that would teach me that. I wanted to become a performer, an actor. So off I went to Paris, with like, just enough money to pay for one term at Lecoq Theatre School. It was amazing but so expensive. I worked in the Metro [Underground] to pay my expenses. I met Columbians and people from Madagascar, Spaniards, and they trained me how to do puppets. I started to do puppets and that's how I supported myself. I moved thirteen times in three years, because I could never pay rent properly. It sounds really crazy but I did it! I told myself *I just had to stay there.* From there it was this thing of working from silence and I think poetry came from silence, because poetry for me is like music, it's notes of music that you hear in a silence, and when you hear a really good poem there's a silence that comes out and then falls back into that silence. I was writing a little bit of poetry but I was basically exploring my body and performing, sometimes with words but mostly not with words. I think I was incubating the poet that I wanted to become.'

Phillippa came back to South Africa in 1992 when she joined Theatre for Africa which performed nature plays in Asia and Europe. She went on to 'street theatre' and landed a role in a *Molo Fish*, which paid for a breather and the chance to study the Artist's Way, a course in discovering and recovering your creativity.

'I did it for three months, did it very carefully. I did morning pages, everything, and I became a writer over that process. Much of that process is about asking *what do you really want?* And I wanted to have a child and I knew I'd never be able to afford a child as an actress. I needed to be able to do something more solid in the world. So I decided to go back to university and study script writing. And I also fell back on the familiar: whenever I was emotional, I'd write a poem. And then I had my baby, everything according to plan. I was with his father, and I was writing scripts for the SABC. And the more scripts I wrote the more poetry I wrote. And it became a comfortable place to exist. I'd never been connected with people. Writing was a world where I could just be. It was such a relief from being out there in the world in my twenties, just fighting to negotiate a path for myself. I was completely accepted. And then motherhood is such an inspiring place to be, it's so wonderful. But also, I found my [biological] parents and that also helped. That was one of the things I wanted to do before I had a baby. That closed the circle.'

With help from a sympathetic social worker, Phillippa contacted both her mother and father who lived in Adelaide, Australia.

'I dialed international directory enquiries and got my father's number. He answered the phone. That conversation, I'll never forget. It was awkward, he didn't know about me, but he did sort of know about me. And finally I had to ask him, *are you black?* And he laughed, he said, *of course I am, I'm Ghanaian.* His name was Amamoo. He was very friendly, he said, *thanks for coming to find me, I'm very glad that you're back in my life.* And he's just been amazing ever since. We're very close now. I wanted to have that African identity so I asked him to give me a name. He asked me what day I was born on. A Thursday, and that's how I became Yaa.'

We talk about Phillippa's one woman play *Original Skin.*

'I was never able to write down what happened to me: what it meant to be adopted, growing up in this other family, the sense always, that there's something missing, that I didn't belong and I wasn't in the right place. I could never write it in words but I knew how powerful writing could be, how deeply an expression of your soul, and it was only after I had contacted and spoken to my biological parents that I was able to make a whole picture – a beginning, a middle and an end.

'At that time [after the birth of her son] I was writing for TV to earn a living and at night I would write poetry. It was all this confessional poetry, it was like all these experiences, I was finding the words. I was in my thirties and for the first time, I was writing about who I am and where I come from.

'In 2005 I thought, I really wanted to explore this poetry thing. So I entered into a competition run by the British Council and I got into a learnership, a mentorship. It was called "Crossing Borders", and for eight months, I had my own mentor, a British poet called John Lindley. Also he just encouraged me to write. He really helped me because I kept thinking that every thing that I wrote that was personal, was just therapy and shouldn't be seen by any one. And he said to me, *where would Sylvia Plath be if we thought like that?*'

'Lindley affirmed me and also led me to other writers. He led me to Jackie Kay, a black, transracial adoptee and an amazing writer. She wrote a play called *Adoption Papers.* I read that play and I just felt like I wanted to own my own story and tell the story. But it was only in engaging with poetry, really going into poetry that it happened – within six weeks of working with John I wrote a first draft of my whole life story. It contained things I'd heard around the braai from white people who assumed I was one of them. I entered it into a play writing competition in Durban. *Where the children live* won two awards and quite a lot of money, even though it was quite difficult to stage! And during this time I got involved with Jozi House of Poetry run by Myesha Jenkins. She's American and basically she ran sessions that were very female friendly because a lot of poetry sessions are very male dominated and it's very difficult to be vulnerable in a space like that.

'I went to these sessions to read and recite my poetry and these women said, *wow, this is great!* And they invited me to read on other platforms. But it was quite an amazing thing, reading my own poetry. I felt so exposed, how can I describe it . . . I felt as though I was having my skin stripped off me. And I was growing in a way that I'd never imagined. This exposure to a group of poets – Myesha, Khosi Xaba, Napo Masheane, Lebo Mashile – made me feel like I was part of a movement where women were telling their stories. It was really affirming.'

Phillippa explains how wrestling with the poetry and stage symbolism of her life story, how a basic desire to protect her adoptive parents, slowly evolved into the one woman, self performed play, *Original Skin*. Directed and co-written by Robert Colman, the play traveled around South Africa and to Germany.

'How do you get your ideas for poetry, how do you capture them?'

'In different ways. Some of my poems are read, like I say let's just write this poem now. Those are the ones I don't really trust but there are others where I feel . . . sometimes they come, it's like an itch, you can only scratch it by writing it down. And then you don't even know what you've written. You have no idea what it is. I think it's because it's been so tied up with my healing process as a person, and I doubt those ones too. I guess because of theatre, I've got this idea that you must respect people, if you're taking them away from their own process, you must give them something that's worth their while, you know. So I have to really try to trust my processes as relevant to other people too. And I think the poems about adoption were like, there's the emotional pain that conjures lots of images and then there's the critical part, which is when you read it and go, *okay, does this hang together, how can I say this better?* And sometimes I write three or four poems in one outpouring. And then I really have to trust it's okay to take that stuff out and to extract things and to craft the poem, you know. I love it, I love it so much, because it's like acting, when I write I'm trying to give you a present, I want to be this close to you when you read my poetry, I want you to smell my breath, well [giggles furiously]. Poetry is a very hard road. It's a very hard, lonely, mystical experience. Poetry demands integrity, It demands a certain sense from you and then that becomes your focus, it becomes your shirt and then, writing, when it's not from that space that feels true to you, becomes very difficult.

□

I chose this poem because it was one of the first I wrote about being adopted, more than 16 years after that I was told that I was adopted. It was after I went to see the Princess Alice Home, where I lived for the first 10 months of my life. I couldn't get to the feeling somehow, it was out of reach – it was so long ago. I had to imagine what it might have meant. I was experimenting with a Japanese poetic form called haiban.

Wanting

Infants don't remember: I can't recall
the rough blanket of the nurse's love bundled out
in bulk to the babies 'awaiting placement';
the metal deafness of
her pen, charting our progress, our feeding and faeces:
all of this is gone. Her kind indifference,
like the white bars of our cots,
confining each of us to our
clean, dry, comfortable, solitary cells;

may or may not have been there.
I might have made it up.
She might have cared.
I don't remember giving up crying or
ever wanting for anything,
except that I did always want something,
besides the usual
milk and material.
(Good stuff, but not enough).
I think maybe what I wanted and what I want
Is to remember,
that's all,
remember my story clearly.
My mind is a hand reaching out to trace
the features of a forgotten face:

Waves retreat, expose
the beach; naked snails and crabs
sucking and pinching.

☐

*This was the first time I attempted to address social issues alongside
personal ones. It was also the first overtly oral poem, although I think that
all poems are initially oral, this one has a kind of clarion ring to it, and it
was very popular.*

Tea for Thabo

I invited our president to tea, I said
I have issues with your take on identity
so bring along your kneepads, it's going to be a bumpy ride.

He arrives in a shiny 2002 Rhetoric with
white leather seats. Metaphoric
because a motor car's now equivalent to black pride.

But pride lies in acacia shade
flicking flies, watching you with yellow hunter's eyes,
pride is too wild to be racial.
A silence is a contest: who will win?
usually not the person who begins.

I say, Thabo, or should I say, Mr M,

you've bartered the freedom charter for a full house BM
and the corolla-ry to this theory
is to be or not to be a Z-3.
And the people? We cream our
fongkong jeans, zama zama,
thatha ma chance.
But who's taking?
Who's chancing?

He says: "the way forward is to level the playing field
to wield the consumer power.
Let's face it, at the end of the day,
to be black is to have suffered.
Cash is the salve for the nation
so don't come with your half-baked theories of liberation."

Ayeye ... I feel the labour coming on:
My Volvo! Audi!!!
The waters have broken the damn wall,
the have-nots are flooding the metropole,
contractions coming four by four!
And you're so Anglo-Saxon
reaching for the klaxon,
calling cops,
locking doors,
red ants crawling over
the repossessed possessions of the
dispossessed.

Too late!
Congratulations!
You're the father of a healthy brothel nation.
Uncle America will come over her,
Auntie Europe will knit her a nice fleecy trade policy
and she looks just like you
except for the car.
Aunt Asia who used to be so far
now owns the corner, trash piled like a scar.

Leaders defend us, doesn't matter who you are.
Some leaders are Mercedes, others Jaguar.
I didn't fight to be freed,
to give you a license for greed.

He turns on me with a sudden speed.
"You whites get so cross when we blacks succeed.
Why don't you just go back
to where your ancestors come from?"
Aha! Now I'm white!
My race is now a slur
but the boundaries are blurred because I…

I am the product of three centuries of cross-border… shopping.
Horse-trading, cattle thieving, dipping into gene pools,
swapping stories, swapping schools,
a highland fling, Ashante.
You can try to shut the stable door,
call back the galloping incidents of past deals and schpiels.
They disappear into dust.
We sit in the ashes of our history
ready to make our contribution:
life is our inheritance,
speaking out, our retribution.

I can't look back to a time when everything was perfect.
I can only look forward to a time when everything could be perfect.

A silence becomes uncomfortable after the third beat.
So much for dialogue with the elite:
he clears his throat and departs.
Well, you can't end a conversation that never really starts.

I look out of the window at the sunset.
Joburg hospital, the black line of the incinerator chimney
exhaling burnt blood and dressings into the smouldering sky.

Perfect.
Perfect is the puzzle, the piece that never fits,
a story never finding, never winding down.
Peace.

□

*Tissue Paper doesn't have the power of **Tea for Thabo** nor its significance, but it's also a personal response to the president of South Africa.*

Tissue Paper

When I go to the metropole I feel defensive:
We Africans are not barbaric, I assert.
Meanwhile the TV yells
that we have elected
an alleged rapist
an accused thief
an unashamed polygamist
to the presidency.
I tell them they don't know what it's like:
there are differences in custom and tradition,
loss happens in translation,
these things are also coloured by racism
the west has its pets, its tame Annans,
it's not our fault that you don't understand us –
you never have.

On the flight home, I study the cold
black tablet of the aeroplane window.
Level with the stars, we cruise over Africa
her masses in their thrall of poverty,
their unnegotiated fate.

When I step off the plane, I feel like a missionary.
I want to tell everybody to use a condom,
treat women fairly, get educated, get a life.

Traveling pulls me apart
into soft tissue paper
in layers;
I wouldn't have it any other way.

It's so much easier
to pack the fragile things.

□

Going to Cuba was an incredibly restorative experience. I was able to connect – really connect – my social self and my inner self, my closest family, my political ideals. I don't think I'd ever been able to celebrate and honour a family relationship in a very simple way.

Origin

Tonight,
my son, my favourite poem,
shares my bed.
His gentle snores like footprints on the night.
He is upside down. What dream
is holding him
by the ankle?
It has been two weeks and 10 000 miles,
our skins and eyes separated from one another.
Mothers and their sons inhabit each other differently.
We are more than milk; we are also
bread and the law and desire.
I know that
I am his home, as much as he is
my shelter. I am an expanding house,
growing taller as he reaches past me for
his own life.
Che Guevara changed the world for me. He was
some mother's son who dreamt a fairer future.
Our breakfast is our ideals, what we want
the world to be, most important of the
meals; and life, the greatest prize, we fight
in trenches to defend its sovereignty.
This is how I was born in blood and
pain and mortality, my mind bright,
laughing up to wish for more, and force
my tired feet against the discouraged hill,
and harness my rage and ride it home to change,
and still return to that first poem that called me
       Mama.

Ike Mboneni Muila

Prologue

Originally, Ike wanted to be an actor, training at Funda Centre, then the Market Theatre Laboratory. He was put through his paces by professionals such as Vanessa Cooke and John Kani. He'd spend the week working and dossing down in the Market workshop and then return home to Soweto on weekends. He'd bring enough money each week to see him through to Friday. One rainy evening he set off to Fontana in Jeppe St, nearby, to buy supper. He was mugged by a gang who took his money, beat him about the head and additionally, tried to break his neck, leaving him for dead on the pavement. Many people walked by, ignoring what they thought was Ike's corpse. Eventually someone discerned breathing and called for help. Ike spent a long time in Charlotte Maxeke hospital and later in rehab. He was unable to act again in any major way, due to what was explained to him, as a brain injury stroke. It was then that he turned more particularly to creative writing and poetry. His life would probably have been very different as a professional actor, but he sees his injury in a positive way; as an opportunity to open another major door. As Ike says, "After my 'accident', it was a heavy time for me but with the help of my friends consoling me, instead of despairing, it became a new turning point."

Allan Kolski Horwitz drives Ike to my house where Ike and I sit down before the tape recorder to hear his story. I ask where his poetry began.

'Initially I started when I went to an African stage/drama school at Diepkloof Funda Centre under Soyinkwa Institute of African theatre. That is where I met with the marimba music students preparing for an open public performance. They invited me into their rehearsal and asked me to prepare a Tshivenda poem from the library for the performance. So I went to the library to read the writers of a long time ago to select poems that I could present and perform, and that's how I started. As a student of stage/drama I combined my acting skills and creative writing in order to fit in as a performance poet otherwise I believe that I am flexible in both reading and performing because of the acting skills that I learnt. Prose or no prose creative writing came about as I was attending open classes of creative writing facilitated by the then professor Hezekia Mphahlele.

'And when I went to the Market Theatre Laboratory, that's where I met other writers. I was fascinated by what these writers were doing but I also wanted to show them a few things that I could do, especially when it comes to poetry. In my style I mix languages. I write in Isicamtho which combines several South African languages including the so-called Tsotsitaal which is now used much in the media like radio, TV, especially in advertisements. In Isicamtho we use 'heita' when greeting or 'hola' as it is in Venezuela where they say 'hola' when greeting. Isicamtho strives to bring people and languages together.'

I ask Ike whether he'd primarily call himself a performance poet.

'Not necessarily. I started as a creative writer, as a student of drama. In fact, our tutor told us that we shouldn't wait for the director or writer to write something for us to perform, we should also learn the craft of writing. When I'm asked if I'm a poet I grin from ear to ear. I'm just a creative writer.'

'Was that creative writing in prose?'

'It was not actually prose but a way of expressing myself and a way of looking at the poetry of other writers. Looking at those before me, how do they write? And also so as not to put myself in a certain box or genre, I wanted to set myself up to become a better creative writer, better in any kind of writing. I believed that for me to be more creative it would be by reading other writers, reading intensely but not copying, inciting myself to bring out the better me. Reading helped me to understand the world around me, going around with open eyes, the mind's eye, seeing things and trying to keep languages alive.'

We go back to Ike's development as an actor/writer at the Soyinkwa Institute.

'Our tutors told us we would do prescribed plays and also our own workshopped plays. One of our workshopped plays was on the plight of the elderly people when they go to get their pension money: long queues, people fainting, people being robbed. So we made our research and decided to title our play *Mdala*, meaning an elderly person. 'Madala' in Isicamtho means a close friend, a person whom you can easily associate with. 'I also wrote a poem when I arrived at the Market Theatre Laboratory. I called it *Blomer Madala* which in Isicamtho means 'Hang Around'. It's advice to old people that they shouldn't give up but hang on and fight against the odds. It was published together with other poems I wrote at the time.'

I ask Ike whether politics has greatly influenced his poetry.

'Umm, yes and no. Yes in the way of Isicamtho. Isicamtho came about because our parents came into Johannesburg as migrant workers. Some from Lesotho, others from Venda, they came to work here. Isicamtho is different from Fanagalo which was used on the mines. Isicamtho was a way of communicating in a common language among migrants who came from all over the country. It was used by those who were removed from Sophiatown. It used some elements of Tsotsitaal here and there, together with a mixture of other languages. It was a way of expressing oneself, a means of communicating amongst each other. Even though the oppressor was around, he couldn't understand you. All he could do was laugh at the beauty of the language. It was a secret language, a code among the comrades.

'Now I use many languages but with Isicamtho, that was my way of learning other people's languages. My mother tongue is Venda but I was first educated in Zulu. I grew up meeting and playing with kids from different language groups – Zulu, Sotho, Xhosa. So when I realized the beauty of writing in a mixture of languages it became an inborn sickness to me. I can't finish a verse without mixing the language in between. Ja, even when I was speaking, sometimes I would put in a word from another language. When someone says, how are you, Ike? I say lovely, 'moja, moja'. It's not like proper English, it's a different tale altogether from another language. We address each other in terms of, he is my colleague, he is my peer. It's not the same as when I address my own kids. I address them in a semi-formal way.'

I ask Ike when he started mixing English into his poems.

'English came later, round about '97/'98, when I was at Funda Centre. Mixing is a way of preserving languages, including Afrikaans. It's a language that was born here at home. Because, if you go to Holland, nobody understands Afrikaans so much, they will tell you, noo . . . [laughs] . . . when you go to England you find that the English standard there is different to the English that we speak here. So mixing languages, it preserves languages so they remain alive all the time. I also use English, mind you not to abuse it, but as a driving force vehicle behind all our languages, official en unofficial. In an association of Isicamtho words with English it simplifies the logic for my readers en audience, helps them to find it and understand without complaints or asking for the translation except when the need arises. In fact, mixing languages and English with me started even before I knew it while I was at the Soyinkwa Institute. When we put up workshopped plays we were using all eleven languages in diversity including Tsotsitaal, mix motion theatre pieces addressing the plight of elderly and other people.'

I ask whether Ike's listeners and readers ever complain that there are too many languages in his poetry, making it very difficult to understand.

'I never came across a problem like that even when I was in England [Ike performed at the Cambridge poetry festival in 2005] after I came back from Berlin [where he performed in 2004]. Others were having their work translated before they went to present their work but in my case they said no, we understand because it's become performance and what you say doesn't need a translator. Because as a performance poet when I deliver, I make sure that I treat the audience in such a way that they don't ask for translation. I use words to make a person understand; it doesn't help to look for a dictionary. And I also use body to show what I'm saying.'

'There's an actor working in there?'

'Yes.'

I ask Ike about the poetry he's published.

'We formed a performance group, Botsotso Jesters. We also started to publish and do other things for ourselves and for other poets. I had my first poetry collection *Gova* published with the help of funds from the Roy Joseph Cotton Poetry Trust. This was before going to the Cambridge poetry festival. But then we had so many other books that we published as Botsotso Jesters – books like *We Jive Like This*, *Dirty Washing* and *Greetings Emsawawa*. In the group we write collective poems addressing the social issues happening at present and in the past. And then we share stanzas; each one of us writes a full stanza, and another a full stanza, and we bring it together using Botsotso Jesters as a bridging gap, passing on to each one amongst ourselves. When you are published that's when one feels fulfilled en accepted by all in the creative writing fraternity. I don't believe so much in a finish complete on the spot or a quick fix kind of creative writing just like that from a stroke of a pen. We all strive for excellence though perfection is something else that should otherwise be left in the hands of the Almighty Creator.'

I ask about the formation of Botsotso, the poetry collective, which once was a larger group but now comprises Ike, Siphiwe ka Ngwenya and Allan Kolski Horwitz.

'Some dropped out and others passed on. Like the lady who I used to perform with at the poetry festivals in Grahamstown, Isabella Motadinyane. We were performing somewhere round '90 and '92. We used to go Grahamstown and perform on the fringe. Me and Isabella, we used to combine our poetry with music. We didn't play a musical instrument – we believed our voices were the instruments. We performed folk songs, songs that belong to the people not a certain individual who had composed and written them. We were like recreating the folk songs and formalizing them. We sang working songs, religious songs but later some of our creative writing songs. One would do his poem, then the other one would do a poem, then we'd sing a song and then, only to find that someone was watching us. And when we came back home after the Festival we received a letter from Allan [Kolski Horwitz]. 'Hey, guys, why don't we come together and start a poetry collective?' And then we started doing performance poetry live; meanwhile writing stanzas in between. And seeing the possibility of recording our poetry and then publishing other poets; keeping alive the up-and-coming writers.

'You know how difficult it is to get published.' I add, 'And how great it is when you are published.'

'We met with Allan and we sat down and we said we know such and such poet, he's a good performer, we can invite him to be in the group. We started with quite a number and we ended up five. It was Allan, myself, Siphiwe, Anna Varney and Isabella. When we first published the magazine, in 1994, we started with an insert in a newspaper called New Nation. They helped us spread the word and attract other young writers. On the other hand, me and Siphiwe used to go to Newtown. There were two places for poetry – the Horror Café and Kippies. Every month we'd go there and read our creative writing. Every month I had something new so that when I read I got feedback from the audience. How did they receive my work? They were coming to talk to me: how do you do this? How sure are you that you now have a poem in your hand? So I tell them when you write and when you read intensely and you do something that you love, you must love it yourself before you can expect somebody else to love it for you or to appreciate it.

'If it's so inside you and you really love what you're doing, definitely for sure, people will receive it well. Not everybody will appreciate it, but writers, they don't criticize your work destructively, they criticize your work constructively. Ja, because as a writer myself I don't believe in a completed work. I'm always getting feedback from audiences and other writers and then I go back to my work and allow it to grow. I don't believe in a finished draft on the first go. I've got to give it time to sort of grow, ja. And I've got to be selective in the words that I use, it doesn't matter if I'm using Tsotsitaal or a mixture of languages, it's the imagination of words. And how I'm using the word from the paper to the stage, that's important also, it counts a lot. Once you're inspired, you've got to give yourself time, show everything that comes in your mind and work on that until you are happy inside, until you are satisfied, my work is good, than I can go and open myself to criticism and be able to accept the reaction of people. Not everyone will be one hundred per cent on your side, some will be on the other side and they will be showing you where you are lacking.'

We turn to the 'mixture of writers' from whom Ike drew inspiration. He doesn't remember too many names but rather their influence.

'Whenever I feel like writing something, I should go and do some reading and get that urge of writing whatever I want to write from reading others. And when I joined the Congress of Writers [COSAW}, they were still here in Fordsburg, they used to show DVDs of poets from different places. Langston Hughes, an American poet, used to read his poems with music, jazz music. I liked the way he performed the poem *I have known rivers big and small*. I also liked the Jamaican poet Mutabaruka and the British poet LKJ (Linton Kwesi Johnson).

'I thought the COSAW would be like a home for writers but the politics, eh, one could not escape really. It can shatter one's dreams of going further into something that one loves. So, I didn't know what happened, it never lived to the expectations of people as a home for writers. When I was doing my practicals in acting at the Market Theatre, I had an accident [as described in the prologue], but I found that I could force that into creative writing, following renowned writers. So I had something to fall back on as I slowed down in terms of acting.'

I ask Ike whether he's always struggled with money.

'Yes, yes, I did. When you are doing something that you love most . . . You know I started a small, small spaza. I buy and sell cold drinks and loose draw nkauza skyf for smokers. Because of the laws we live under I become careful not to sell to children. I sell only to elderly people and am careful not to sell cigarettes that are smuggled into the country. I've been running the spaza, I can say, since 2000. My son and my daughter-in-law and the two grandchildren are living with me. My son did not finish his degree in economics and computers. He lives by doing temporary jobs. In the yard he has a hair saloon, so the living is better because of his work. Sometimes there's a little extra if one is lucky enough to receive a call to a poetry performance that pays. Meanwhile I'm trying my level best to make ends meet en up to scratch without waiting for a call from the blue.'

'So you keep on with poetry?'

'I love the poetry in that it makes me fulfilled inside. I can't really stop. You see somewhere somehow it's inevitable. It's like stopping to breath. Money or no money, one cannot stop to breath. Poetry makes me tick en brightens my day. Like calling sound bells it awakens my aimless wandering mind. I enjoy poetry more than a person who is enjoying a ntofo-ntofo sponge cake. I also hear that some poets offer themselves for hire but I reward myself. I'm not part of that business. That kind of thing kills the really creative person inside you. There's a saying in African language that a person is a person only because of another person – Ubuntu. And for myself to become who I am, it's because I've been influenced by others. I've learnt from the ones who came before me so I'm keeping the torch burning for whatever.

'One day I was with my granddaughter. I was practicing a poem and mixing the poem with a song: *Baby Don't Cry*. And she started singing too. What was she doing if not letting me know I could pass on, that she would still appreciate me even if I'm not here. And that's another reason to keep on, that's another reason to keep the words coming.'

*Isabella Motadinyane once asked me when i was going to write something in English
because writing in the vernac wasn't going to get me anywhere..., i answered that
you have to master your home language first and foremost and then you'll be able to
master other languages..., in this poem i'm showing i'm at home in all of them and that
Scamtho is my answer to the question of which South African language should be used.*

BUDDY SCAMTHO

Eers ek moet mense groet ka motswako	*First I must greet people (Afrikaans)*
	With this mixture (Sotho)
Scamtho wise..,we molo	*As far as Scamtho goes...,*
	Hello! (Xhosa)
abusheni halo	*How are you? (Tsonga)*
mangwanani	*Greetings! (Shona)*
sanibonani	*How are you? (Zulu)*
thovhela ri ya losha	*Hello! we greet you! (with*
	clapping of hands) (Venda)
hasalaam alaikum	*Peace be with you! (Arabic)*
malaikum salaam	*(Response) and peace be with you!*
welele ebukhosini bakhiwa	*Salutations, your highness (Zulu)*
	(Scamtho) the kind one
holasharphoezit moja	*(Scamtho) Hi, great,how you*
	doing? fine
luister nou mjojo grend grend moja hierso	*listen now very carefully,*
tweede	*everything here is fine, just tops*
matakadza mbilu; ndi nwana	*happiness in the heart is a child*
matakadza mbilu ; ndi nwana	
chu chu baby ; ndi nwana	*cry cry baby is a child*
chu chu baby ; ndi nwana	
buddy scamtho	
first and fore most I accept and thank you	
for your invitation	
with my most humble beginnings	
buddy scamtho jam	
nwana mme smoko	*child of mother smoke*
kasi prent shosholoza style	*carry on location movie style*
khoma switiya nwana mmani	*hold on tight my mother's child*
spikiri hammer chisel foloza mkokoteli	*nail hammer chisel follow up driver*
dish dash pozi jinda warm ginsa laphasite	*dish-dash home let alone hot*
	stolen property

52

skokkende werk liyashisa emsawawa cowsin   *frightful work its hot in south*
                                           africa bullish coward

i am into creative writing as a poet artist performer
my narrative oral mix is in eleven
languages spoken in south Africa
by en bye trapped in one poem
the so-called tsotsitaal isicamtho lingo alive...,

en kicking sense of humour in you en me
mixing of languages into a witty lingo
a language of identity
a language of an ordinary person in the street
a language of unity in diversity

matakadza mbilu; ndi nwana
matakadza mbilu; ndi nwana
chu chu baby; ndi nwana
talk talk baby; ndi nwana
cry cry baby; ndi nwana
oh; oh; baby; ndi nwana
matakadza mbilu ndi nwana
matakadza mbilu ndi nwana

a song matakadza mbilu is a folk song by
the malende dance culture which says what brings
happiness to the heart is a child
in this instance
the ultimate child
in my case
is isicamtho

The poem Blomer marked my turning point into creative writing fulltime. What inspired me was that while in the then Hillbrow Hospital when i woke up from the unknown in the ICU i grabbed the doctor by the jacket en asked him about my pack of cigarettes.., now people who paid me a visit, i mean everyone who come to see me with food parcels ,i asked them to bring me cigarettes en from that pack i would smoke one when i woke up in the morning en another one after lunch en the third one before i went to sleep, that way i was saving for the next visit cause i wasn't sure who en when is the next visitor coming with another packet of cigarettes..,

BLOMER

blomer	*Hang around*
blomer madala	*hang around old buddy*
ek is 'n ou taxin terries	*I'm an old texan town*
binne in die toene	*inside my toes*
change deurdlana	*changing door to door*
op en af	*up and down*
blomer madala	*hang around buddy of mine*
blomer jozi	*hang around Joburg*
blomer joburg	*hang around city Joburg*
jakarumba spy vanity logo	*vanity logo foolish spy*
big short kota	*big short quarter*
four five limited tamtasie	*four five limited witty case*
ek ken jou haba witty madala	*i know you are not wise buddy*
haba stalavisto	*no by the by*
niks ou medulla oblongata	*nothing like witty medulla oblongata*
blomer	*hang around*
blomer madala	*hang around buddy of mine*
ek spin in die toene ek nou die dag	*i spin inside my toes these days*
jy sal never nie skarf kry nie	*you will never receive a smoke from me*
check lapha site	*check this side*
calaza madala site	*peep cautiously this side*
ek vang hulle is net dresh	*i believe there are three only*
die een…, is 'n ou mdryseni	*this one is for while away time*
die ander een…, is 'n ou malala	*the other one for when it's time to sleep*
die laaste een…, is 'n ou mavuka	*the last one for when i wake up*
jy moet onthou	*you should bear in mind*
skyf is 'n process	*pass me a smoke is a process*
whereby cigarettes	*whereby cigarettes pass*
passes from the owner to the parasite	*from the owner to the parasite*
blomer	*hang around*
blomer madala	*hang around old buddy*

A dedication poem to bra Frisco wonke-wonke Mukosi Muila.., a poem which was inspired by stories of Sophiatown (Kofifi); how families en my family members were forcibly relocated to the present day Mofolo village (Soweto) in 1955 before i was born.., en how my father refused to stay in Ndofaya (Meadowlands) en decided to settle in Mofolo central where there is a mix of people not only Vendas on their own..., en how my brother wonke-wonke got his name Frisco in some shebeen drinking slot people drinking on him as if drinking a Frisco coffee to quench their all night long party hangover..,

To bra Frisco Mukosi Muila

Born in 1945/02 /01 laid to rest at Tshiheni, near Lake Fundudzi 2011/03/12

mukosi wo lila thavhani	*an outcry over the mountains*
ha da na vha si nongo da	*there came even those who never come before*
wonke wonke Frisco kofi	*everyone likes Frisco coffee*
linothile liya fudumalisa	*it's rich and warming*
kanti lisheshe likuenzele kalula	*on the other hand it's easy to brew*
one thing for sure	*one thing for sure*
haba niks is fokolo is niks	*having nothing is nothing to worry about*
my mma se kind	*my mother's child*
net `n oomblik	*just a little while*
ek sal julle notch	*i will see you*
in no time spot on	*in no time spot on*
bra Frisco kofi	*brother Frisco coffee*
jika jive malombo jazzman	*dance ancestors jazzman jive*
boeda buddy van my	*buddy brother of mine*
wasemzini is waar	*from home indeed*
jolly tai-tai	*jolly tycoon*
my mma se kind	*my mother's child*
ta Frisco kofi dascholar	*brother Frisco coffee the scholar*
Sophiatown ship twist	*Sophiatown ship twist*
endofaya kusuka amaphepha	*in Meadowlands out fly papers*
kusala amakhadibox	*cardboard boxes remain behind*
kwa ndonga ziyaduma	*where walls shake and tremble*
inyama ayi pheli	*meat cannot be finished*
kuphela amazinyo endoda	*only man remain without teeth*
boeda buddy Frisco kofi	*buddy brother Frisco coffee*
van ons dak nie	*of we have no where to go*
ons phola hierso	*we stay here*
pf gandakanda hangover	*tractor face drunkard hangover*
stoki hurrah	*come together stocky party hurrah*
white pepper poetry fuss food	*white pepper poetry fuss food*
go down crazy in my system	*go down crazy in my system*
cockeye gist brown ginger cake	*cockeye gist brown ginger cake*
hurting my consumption capacity	*hurting my consumption capacity*
heke.., kha la venda	*venda ok.., right*

This poem is about an old game, Musangweni, the BaVenda bare fist fighting. These fights take place when people are taking cattle to the dip and men and young boys, according to their age and size, challenge each other. No women are allowed to watch. Some professional boxers started out playing this game and this is why there is now a move to revive it. Funnily enough the chant niyabasabana, hayi asibasabi siyabafuna is used at soccer matches by Vendas and non-Vendas alike.

DUBE

vhaya delela vhafana	boys are bullies
vhaya delela	they are bullies
niyabasabana	do you fear them?
hayi asibasabi siyabafuna	no, we don't fear them – we challenge them
fear go	fear go
fear fight	fear fight
fear go…,	fear go…,
buddy rough dance tshilendele	buddy rough dance a persistent coward
tshitamba na vhasidzana	playing with girls
hofsite wrong site daas nie plek	above site wrong site there's no place
for sweet lekkerheid bugger rol hier so nie	for sweet nothing bugger all here any more
bafana bafana	boys will be boys
fear go	fear go
fair fight	fair fight
fear go…,	fear go…,
hayi bamba hayi luma bhari	no holding no biting fool
I hate mazondi phangas	i hate stones machetes
goni bhaxaza down	knife gun down
shake hands steady gongsplit	shake hands steady gongsplit
rumble roar in the jungle maseven	rumble roar in the jungle holy seven
fear go	fear go
fair fight	fair fight
fear go…,	fear go…,
los my cherry shaluza saratoga express	leave my girl alone careful Saratoga express
magwa dzia nyendela tshilendele	you step on my toes and its war persistent coward
tshitamba na vhasidzana	playing with girls

welele	*who's next*
wele wele wela wela	*so rush over*
fear go	*fear go*
fair fight	*fair fight*
fear go…	*fear go…*

□

I was once invited to a poetry workshop at Ipelegeng during the time an American hip hop poet visited us…, at the workshop she asked us to write a poem about anything we liked but that we must first look out the window and then write…, i wrote this poem but it was only when i got home that i really worked on it – really looked inside myself. The next day i read it over and over again and only then did i put the last touches. The subject matter is about things i used to do and the criticisms that friends would offer me – like going out and drinking alcohol without first eating, and mixing drinks which caused me to vomit. All these things came back to me – these things which i wanted to outgrow…, one glass of wine is now more than enough!

INSIDE OF ME

inside of me joe	*inside of me joe*
the language stream	*the language stream*
all assorted jolly eat en be merry	*all assorted jolly eat and be merry*
moonlight stars milk shake	*moonlight stars milk shake*
bazabaza witness above	*huge witness above*
inside of me	*inside of me*
there is no room for cappuccino	*there is no room for cappuccino*
home made brew en beers collide	*home made brew and beers collide*
causing me to vomit	*causing me to vomit*
inside of me joe	*inside of me joe*
barekesa malana le mohodo	*they are selling cow tripes inside meat*
madombolo le magwinya	*dumplings and fat cakes*
oesophagus colour bar print slow down	*oesophagus colour bar print slow down*
jabs langsaan	*jabs nearby*
inside of me joe	*inside of me joe*
sponge lungs chicken bean bones	*sponge lungs chicken bean bones*
flat tubes archer ginger cake spinza oven	*flat tubes archer ginger cake liquor oven*
grey	*grey*
time tick tock ticks drum turn	*time tick tock ticks drum turn*
fantastic orange heart beat yo yo flex	*fantastic orange heart beat yo yo flex*
inside of me	*inside of me*
some one is knocking passionately	*some one is knocking passionately*
to no avail	*to no avail*
sour kidney structure four five draw	*sour kidney structure four five draw*
six nine appeal get mchovana	*six nine appeal get by*
rovers reff hum eh..,	*rovers reff hum eh..,*
huks vrystaat	*huks free state*
siphuma kanje..,	*we quit this way*

Gail Dendy

I arrive one very hot afternoon at Gail Dendy's typically renovated house in Parkhurst. She answers the door looking very informal and cool. It appears that she doesn't carry a gram of extra weight. The interior is a model of neat efficiency for hard-working Gail and her husband. I'm introduced to two cats. The third is too shy to make an appearance. We take glasses of cold water to her study where we start quite conventionally.

'Gail, how did you come to poetry?'

'I came to poetry in two different ways, the first, is that I've always written. I started when I was about eight years old. I'd jot down little rhyming things about teachers or whatever, people at school, but the point at which I really tried to write poetry, rather than just writing, was in high school. The thing is, we did poetry as part of English and we were doing all these analytic essays about poems … and the fact is I never believed a single word I was writing. I'd always do well, but we were being taught to 'squeeze out' the lines one by one to see what could be got out of them. And I got to thinking: surely someone writing a poem wouldn't think this way, they wouldn't think, *am I going to put alliteration in line one, am I going to rhyme lines three and four?* So to me, it seemed like I was looking at poetry the wrong way round. So I thought, now let me focus on trying to write poems myself and see what the process is. And that's where it really started, from standard eight [Grade 10] right through to university. 'So,' I say, 'you moved from the analytic to the functional, to the doing?' 'Yes, and I actually learned so much by the doing, filling in 'the other' part of the puzzle. It's good to have both skills, the analytic and the creative – they definitely complement each other.'

'At that time round about matric, you were writing poetry. Was someone helping you, did you have a mentor or were you on your own?'

'Totally on my own; in fact I didn't even admit to people that I was writing poetry because I thought I'd be very much out of it, out of sync with people. It was almost like a dirty secret that I carried around with me [laughter].'

'Where were you at school?' '

'Actually I'm from Durban, so I went to Northlands Girls' High School in Durban North, because I lived right opposite the school. Then I went to university in Natal, Durban and then to the Pietermaritzburg campus. After that I worked at Unisa, and finally I studied through Wits, so I've been everywhere.'

I tell Gail that somehow I'm under the impression that she's a lawyer. Not so; she realized after a year of postgraduate LLB studies that she 'definitely didn't want to be a lawyer.' But the legal knowledge didn't go to waste: she works as a legal research librarian for the Johannesburg office of an international law firm.

'Let's step back to your "dirty secret" – you wouldn't reveal that you were writing poetry at Northlands Girls' High. When did you reveal it; when did you start publishing poetry?'

'Oh, gosh, among the first things that I published were in EAR, the *English Academy Review*. A friend of mine was working in the English Dept at Unisa. And he said *oh, why don't you submit some poems?* So I did and they were picked up on by Ivan Rabinowitz, he was the editor of EAR, and later became head of department. He said *wow, these are fabulous* and he published those. And then my husband, who was a legal academic, had a sabbatical and we went to live in London for a year. I needed a focus for myself, so I decided to write a book of poems and send it to publishers in London. Which is what I did. I didn't know who published poetry in London but you could buy the *Macmillan Writer's Handbook* which gave a list of small, specialist poetry presses. I chose one called 'Diamond Press', figuring that what with diamonds and their connection to South Africa, it should be lucky! So I sent off the manuscript and got a very polite postcard back saying *we don't publish poetry but incidentally I* [the writer Geoffrey Godbert] *am part of another press, Greville, that does publish poetry. I like your work, and so does my fellow editor* [Anthony Astbury], *but there's a third editor.* They said they'd come back to me. As it turned out, the third editor was Harold Pinter. They said *you got a three out of three approval* (which was apparently very unusual). So they published *Assault and the Moth* as a pamphlet. (The Americans call it a chapbook.) Getting published by Harold Pinter was like, WOW! It was totally out the blue. Ironically I'd always been very passionate about Pinter's work. I did a Drama Honours degree and I never thought for a minute … I knew he'd written some poetry, but didn't know he was a publisher. So I was just really, really lucky.'

I started this interview by asking Gail how she came to poetry. But now, taking this a step further, I ask why poetry rather than another form.

'I think because for me an emotion is just so intense, so the only way I can encapsulate and distill it is in the poem format. And also, you know, there's my love of language, that heightened form of language that you can use in a poem. With prose . . . if you tried to do that in a novel it would be so over the top. I was just very drawn to poetry. I love poetry, I love the rhythms of the language. You can be much more particular with rhythms in a short line than you can in prose. For me it just came very naturally.'

I ask whether Gail's poetry was guided by her parents.

'Not at all! I think my father was dyslexic. He readily understood but his verbal reading wasn't good. He read Time magazine and books on true crime. My mother read historical novels and some science fiction. Neither of them was into literature at all, or poetry – definitely not. So the word was this exciting discovery. In Std 7 we did a bit of Shakespeare, that was like WOW! I'm very in love with the language. That year we also did some of DH Lawrence's poems and I went out and I bought my first poetry book ever, a volume of DH Lawrence.'

'So you started really early?'

'I was thirteen.'

We pass on to Gail's regular appearance in the Journal *Carapace*, and I go on to suggest she's become good friends with Gus Ferguson, the publisher.

'Actually, I didn't know him at all when I sent him my manuscript. My second book was *People Crossing*, which Gus published. I don't remember, now, how I got hold of his name and address. Then he phoned one day at some incredibly early hour of the morning, and said *he loved the manuscript, it was everything that poetry ought to be*. Prior to that, I hadn't shown any great amount of poetry to anyone else in South Africa.'

'Are you publishing widely in South Africa now?'

'I try to send to all the journals: *Scrutiny 2, New Coin, New Contrast, Carapace,* those seem to be the major ones. And also to on-line publications, such as *LitNet* and *Incwadi.*'

'Have you won awards?'

'Um, not outright [laughs] ... Oh, I did win the SA PEN Millennium Playwriting Competition, but that was obviously way back when. Regarding poetry, I shared the money from the Herman Charles Bosman Award in 2008. I was shortlisted, and then they said that there'd be no award for that year, but after the ceremony they presented me with a cheque. I shared the prize money with the novelist Niq Mhlongo.'

'Was that for separate poems or a volume?'

'A full-length volume, *The Lady Missionary*, that Kwela published. But then I've been shortlisted and/or a finalist for a lot of other things: oh gosh, the European Union/Sol Plaatje Poetry Prize (twice!), the Thomas Pringle Award (Short Story category), and I've been longlisted for the UK Plough Prize (Poetry) – it was nice to get two poems longlisted in the same year. And then various Readers' Awards ... but I'd really have to look at my CV. I wouldn't say I was out there winning everything going, I certainly haven't. But it's really nice for me when people come up to me, when I've been somewhere or am out doing whatever, and say, *we really like your poetry*. That for me is fantastic, the sort of recognition that makes me feel good.'

'And now a ridiculous question, could you walk away from poetry?'

'Never! And it's interesting you ask that because, just to digress, I thought I'd never get into prose in a big way. I'd written a few short stories and last year I started a novel. I've completed something like forty-four, forty-five thousand words. I want to finish by the end of March [now end January][1]. And the interesting thing is that because I've been very involved with the prose – my 'prose project' I call it – I found that my technique for prose, the bedrock of this technique, comes from my poetry. And I actually realized that having let the poetry slip for some six months in favour of the novel, I'm now feeling very strongly the need to get back to the discipline, because I need that technique. It's quite strange. I never thought that would happen.'

I ask Gail whether this is pure discipline or an emotional need.

'Both! I was missing doing the poetry, because ... I found there're things I couldn't say in prose, and so I'm writing some poems as well, sort of paralleling what I'm doing with the book. It's been very illuminating for me to see how much I *am* tied to poetry, because I didn't know it until I started my prose project.'

'So it's been a sort of double-track progress?'

'Absolutely! It's fascinating, because I never ever expected to have both feelings

---

1 Gail has informed me that the novel is now complete. She is currently in the process of editing it.

and emotions about prose and poetry. And this has highlighted it for me.'

As a keen reader of Gail's poetry in *Carapace*, I tell her that I think I've perceived a shift to the more complex over the past few years.

'No, I don't think so. But it's interesting you say that, because most people following my poetry say it's the other way round. All I know is that my reading has become a lot broader … you know, dipping into a lot more variety. I read a lot of British poetry and also I like foreign poetry in translation … I was reading ancient Chinese poetry at one stage, which for me was like rain on parched earth. I just loved that. So maybe that somehow came together. It's interesting, I really don't know [how my poetry has changed]. I haven't looked at my own writing.'

'Well,' I say, 'it was an impression I obtained.' And I ask Gail again, if she ever benefited from a mentor.

'No, I've been totally on my own and it's been pretty lonely at times. I was sort of hoping, a silly hope I think, that Harold Pinter would maybe want to mentor me, but he wasn't going to mentor anyone, he had his own stuff. You know, I never came across anybody who was in that position, I suppose, other than a teacher in Standard 8 who was complimentary about my school essays. In Std 9 [Grade 11] I entered the inter-school Navy League Essay Competition, completely on my own … no teachers even knew about it … and I got a 'Commended'. But then as I said, I was too scared to show anyone my writing … my poems. So no, it's been totally a voyage of self discovery.'

'How do poems come to you?'

'Well, a lot of them start with a rhythm that arrives in my head … and that leads to a phrase and I'll write that down, but that might well turn out to be in the middle of a poem, not necessarily the first line at all. It's where an emotion comes through, an emotion of a particular rhythm, and a particular 'feel'. It's where the ear engenders itself upon the page. That's the best I can describe it. A lot of my poetry is very personal sounding. I don't write about wars and famine. It's not that I'm not aware of what's happening around me. A lot of my poetry actually is a response to things that have happened. You know, in that first full-length collection, the one that Gus did, one of the poems was based on the murder of two British tourists on an isolated Natal beach. And that became a poem for me. And then there was that awful Van Rooyen character, the paedophile who snatched those six young girls who were never ever seen again. That led to a poem called 'Assault'. So I'm aware of the world but I won't go out and write the specifics about what's actually happening, like specifically those girls who were snatched.'

I venture that Gail's poetry is not necessarily formed by politics.

'No, whenever I've tried to write something political, they turned out to be such bad poems I realized this wasn't for me. But interestingly, in my work I have to be very focused on political, business and legal news, so I'm very plugged in to the world but it doesn't necessarily influence my poetry.' I suggest that the country's politics and social circumstances influence us all to a degree. 'I think so,' says Gail, 'but it's not overt. You're not going to read my poetry and find out what's happening in South Africa. I suppose it's like "the Jane Austen principle"; she's writing about people but isn't assessing the political world in which she was living. And yet I know she was very aware of what was going on. It actually just depends how people approach their poetry. If you want to make the big statements in life, the political and philosophical statements, you can do that . . . I think mine is the quieter, more homely type of writing ... that's the best I can do to explain it.'

'Do you have children?'

'No, not at all, we didn't want [children].'

'You decided not to go that way?'

'Well, yes, and also being a dancer ... it demands a lot from the body. I'd done ballet as a school kid ... like a lot of kids ... and then at university I picked up on contemporary dance – that's my great passion, one of my really great passions. I would've loved to have been a contemporary dancer and I did, I performed up here first with Equinoxe Dance Theatre and later with Robyn Orlin. My main training was with her when I came to live in Jo'burg. And subsequently I've trained at Bat Dor in Israel, Alvin Ailey in New York, and in London I went to London Contemporary Dance Theatre, the night school. I was there for a year. I performed in London as well, a one-off. So my dancing is very, very precious. I still dance – I do ballet classes three times a week with a group of us who've been dancing together for twenty years. You know, dancing, like poetry, is very much informed by rhythm and there's a lot of rhythm in my poetry. I think dancing and poetry work on a parallel path. I've written a few poems about dancing but the crossover is just the issue of rhythm and the emotion, it's the same emotion whether it's coming out in words or in a dance format. I think it's a strange combination because I've never met anyone else who's a poet and a dancer ... a performer. So I've never been able to quite explain it, it's just rather peculiar because the one doesn't dovetail easily with the other.'

'Would you class yourself as a very 'high activity' individual?'

'A very focused, very organized individual, yes. I have to be because I'm also working, but I don't work full-time, but rather part-time, flexi-time, so that allows me the time for dancing and writing and family and housework.'

I ask Gail what happens after a poem has come to her; what is the process from then on?

'I've always followed the same process: I always hand-write the first draft. I usually sit in bed and hand-write ... I've found that's where the ideas start coming, when I'm very relaxed ... we go to bed late, at like midnight. I find that the ideas come to me between finishing up what I need to do for the evening and actually going to sleep, that's my writing time for poetry, not prose. I have to keep a pad at my bedside, because otherwise I'll just switch off the light and eeeee an idea pops into my head. I'm sure you've had the same experience. I can only write with a fountain pen, and it has to be black ink. I'm very particular: it cannot be blue ink. Okay, then I've got my notebook and it gets transposed onto the computer whenever I can, sometime it's the next morning if I've got time, and then there's a very heavy editing process. If you're lucky sometimes a poem just happens, you don't have to do much to it. That sort of thing is wonderful for me, I can virtually send it off. But other poems, it depends on how much the poem needs, it can be days, weeks, months ... and there are certain poems I've been working on for years that just haven't worked out. But I live in hope. That's why I keep my files, so that if I have a dead patch I can go back and select a poem and try to work on it.'

I comment that Gail never throws anything away.

'No, with my computer I'm a poetry hoarder. I still have stuff that was hand-written at varsity. The folder is in a cupboard somewhere. I'm actually scared to look at it again, but if I find it, I won't throw it out, just for my own interest. I did throw out about twenty A4 handwritten diary notebooks, though … it was about ten years ago, when we moved to this house. I'd say I'm a poetry hoarder and a general thrower-out. My husband is a collector, he's always buying new books for his law library and CDs for his music library … he drives me mad because I just want to clear stuff out.'

Towards the end of the interview, I ask Gail if she'd be perturbed if I'd failed to ask her a significant question or questions. After some memory chasing, embracing a rich and varied physical and intellectual life, she says, 'I keep a totally full CV which I never send out, but it's so I can remember all the things that I've done. I've got a list of all the poems I've published, because I can't remember what I sent where, so I've got to have a list. And then there are all my dance performances, because I performed with Robyn for ten years. If you asked me now, I'd say *I don't know, I'd have to look it up*. I've been in so many different spheres that I find it difficult to remember the name of this and that person, you know.' I comment on the extraordinary variety of Gail's life experiences. 'Yes, and as I say, it's why I'm so organized and I suppose why I'm so naturally a librarian, even if I wasn't paid to be a librarian, my books are quite well organized here [at home]. I'm just very orderly … on the one hand, but on the other hand I also have a need to express myself and that's channeled through poetry. As you know when you're writing poetry you put order on to the chaos, the chaos of the broad – the original [draft] – poem.'

I ask Gail about her Jewish Studies teaching.

'Well, as I've said, I grew up in Durban. I went to an ordinary government school where we did RI, "Religious Instruction", and it got to the point where I thought 'I know more about Christianity than I know about my own religion'. So when I got to varsity they offered Jewish Studies at Natal, Durban. It was a one-year course. Interestingly, most of the people doing the course weren't Jewish. It was fascinating! The professor was absolutely dynamic, he was one of the great influences on my intellectual life. What was interesting was that he was the Chief Orthodox Rabbi of Durban. But he never came along with *oh, you just believe*, he would give you a rational and philosophical substratum to everything that he was explaining. He was dynamic, brilliant. So we did a year, and then the authorities turned it into a two-year major. It was a fabulous opportunity. And in that second year I also did Hebrew. That's something I'll go back to when I retire.'

I tell Gail that I'm beginning to perceive her as a great maw, swallowing everything that comes her way [laughter].

'I suppose I just like experiencing life. Not partying, no, not at all . . . I suppose the artistic and the intellectual life, I just love it so much that I want it, I want to experience it. And, you know, growing up here in South Africa I felt so cut off from the rest of the world, especially dancing, but also poetry. Often I still do. So it's that need to find out what's out there. I think that's probably the core of everything. But thank goodness for the Internet, what you can only find there artistically, you know, in terms of poetry and in terms of dance. I can get onto YouTube and see the best dancers in the world who I'll never see live. For me that is like, so exciting.'

Ending, I ask Gail what she's most proud of in her poetic life.

'I'm very proud of Harold Pinter picking up on me ... that was such a big thing, like a transfusion. I've managed to keep the impetus going. When I started, I wondered whether it would peter out ... my ideas and enthusiasm for poetry. It was such unchartered territory, and because I didn't know anybody who was a poet, it wasn't as if I could ask, how does the process develop? I didn't have a clue. I kept at it. So that, I'm proud of. It's not as if poets out there are getting great opportunities and money and whatever. You hope there's someone out there who'll be reading you, but it's not the path to fame and fortune.'

We reflect that apart from external recognition, much of a poet's satisfaction stems from writing a good poem. Does Gail know the difference between her good work and her not-so-good work?

'I'm very censorious of myself and the things I've published. Compared to what I've got on file, maybe it's a quarter to a third that's seen the light of day. I'm my own worst critic, I'm terribly, terribly critical of my work. Sometimes it's a burden, because if you still that inner critic, maybe good things will come out. Part of maturing as a poet is knowing what to spend more time on and what not.'

'Does your husband get involved in your poetry?'

'We have a mutual agreement! I don't read anything he writes, because he writes legal books, and he doesn't read anything I write, because he doesn't "get" poetry. But he's very supportive of my work. I've dedicated several of my books to him.'

I suggest we close with the issue of publicly reading poetry.

'I love performing. When I'm asked to read poetry, I'll do it. And I love it because I can really try to get across what I think a poem means. I do think I perform well. I'm part of a group ... we started working together just over three years ago. We call our performances *Off The Page*. I do poetry, my friend Tony Bentel does music as a pianist, and another friend, Selwyn Klass, drops in prose pieces and puts the programme together. The programmes are fully rehearsed, and we perform them, but with the scripts in front of us, so it's truly taking the words and music 'off the page'. We perform for groups and things like 'Second Innings', which is like the University of the Third Age. At the end of the day, I just love getting my poetry out there. Literature comes more alive when you're sharing it. And that's important to me.'

☐

This is one of my earliest poems (I shudder to think how many decades ago I wrote it), and derives from the days of large, heavy non-digital cameras, tightly coiled rolls of film, darkrooms with their dull red lights, chemicals the smell of which seeped into one's clothes, hair, and fingernails and, finally, the thinnest of wires above one's head on which to clip the soggy prints, hoping they would dry unsullied by any stray particles of dust which could give the subject either 'dandruff' or 'snow'. A young (in those days!) boyfriend had given me his old, scuffed, third-hand Practica SLR, manufactured in Dresden in eastern Germany (when there was an eastern Germany). A kindly fellow student at university taught me how to prise out the film from its little container and to develop the photos, using different techniques and photographic papers to produce a desired effect. I only ever worked with black and white, originally for the sake of economy (the paper and chemicals were cheaper), but later because of the challenge of colouring the world using black, white and ... dare I say it? ... shades of grey.

Developing those photos was, in many ways, akin to writing a poem – the image would begin to show, faintly at first, like a ghost, and then grow through various stages of insubstantiality to solidity. This particular poem, however, is double-sided, just as a photographic image and its negative are a reverse of each other: hence 'love' is simultaneously 'not love', and the imagined closeness becomes imprisonment. And, yes, there are also echoes of the shadows on the walls of Plato's allegorical cave.

Darkroom

You are in my photo
you are luminously held
in my mind
in my mind
in silver images
negative, I shall keep you
secretively dark
in a dust-free room
I shall keep
I shall keep you
devoid of chemicals
and running water
I shall never
I shall never
hang you on lines
hooked up on the slow
on the slow ruby light
of my love
I am jealous
of my love
he is here
he is here
in the dark
in the cave
in my heart.

Gardens have always held a deep fascination for me. In Durban, the fascination was in how they never knew winter. Leaves stayed on the trees. The grass never withered. The sub-tropical climate meant that one could plant all year round, and we did plant, my father and I, working in silence, everything from runner beans and cherry tomatoes to mealies and pumpkins, granadillas to guavas. Moving up to the then-Transvaal was a shock. The vibrant greens of Durban winters were replaced with crisp browns, bleached whites, and even black as the grass burnings took place. I lived in a block of flats, and so my contact with nature was likewise reduced. But the gardens of the flats did have clumps of albizia trees, and I would watch as the trees meticulously produced their feathery, ballet-skirt-like blossoms, and later convert them to dry, hanging pods.

This next poem takes as its genesis the famous poem by William Carlos Williams, 'This is Just to Say'. But whereas his poem is sparse, I've given mine great amplitude. Here and there, another voice breaks into the formal images of poem, one that speaks of wonderment, amazement, that from the dryness of the African earth such life can emerge, a life that encapsulates the tenacity of age.

Whimsy

And this is just to say that

the albizia pods are turning from mild green
to chocolate brown, are lean as slippers,
slightly periwinkle, encrusted
as antique fruits, as jewels.

They are the deepest bass notes
of a seasonal score. *Darling, today I nipped those pods
and found them downy as peaches.*
Their brittle wombs click like maracas,

like disapproving tongues. We, too, have a way
of hiding secrets. The pods are undoubtedly fertile,
those dangling rows of woody, pleated pouches,
dry as dowlings, twisted.

*I can never believe how hardened and sunburned
they are, salt-of-the-earth pods
genteely aging.* They exist in the slowest
of slow motion, in territorial waiting,
are entirely secretive, impregnably smug.

It's near to September. Without my knowing
they've flowered into the greenest spring
between the clumsy hobnails
of early thorns. They are a defiant lot.
Old age, it seems, is hospitable to them.

It's unlikely that any poet has ever avoided writing a love poem. It doesn't seem possible. Perhaps that's because writing about love takes on its own dimensions, its own dynamic, so much so that the words themselves often end up as seeming peripheral. It's almost as though they can get in the way of what one really wants to say.

This next piece is the first part of a five-part poem which deals, very loosely, with my parents' relationship. I can't say I ever knew my parents – not properly, and not well. They were from a generation where the display of emotion was taboo. Or perhaps it was just uncomfortable in a household where the Pinteresque subtext held dominion.

And so this excerpt, below, is a mythical recreation of their courtship. I placed it in the Valley of a Thousand Hills, about an hour's drive inland from Durban, where we would sometimes go for tea on a weekend at the old Rob Roy Hotel. The ups and downs of emotions have been transposed into the landscape – a bird falls and rises, a lane seems to alter in its proportions. But there is an undercurrent of danger: gunpowder, bullets, and poison. As Eliot said, 'In my beginning is my end' (Four Quartets, East Coker). And in a relationship, things of course begin one way, and end in another.

Love Poem

This is the Valley of a Thousand Hills and there
is the single road with rigging lanes, rabbit traps, duck shoots,

where death arrives each year as a squad of reddening berries,
beautiful, high-strung, poisonous. My mother mentioned this place
where she and my father had met, surreptitiously,
under a sturdy and predetermined tree where the lane fizzled

in light rain and dust fanned out like gunpowder
and a bird dropped as if gravity had intensified

but, defying prediction, ascended again, briskly
out of the tree together with its partner, two bullets

drilling at the sky, then vanishing. At nightfall,
my mother said, the lane becomes thinner,

the grassblades longer, everything detailed as if language
could capture it all before it becomes nothing more

than an ordinary, winding, track, which some say
is imaginary and others say is the first beginnings of love.

□

I don't have children, and for as long as I can remember, I never wanted children. That's just how I am. And for most of my adult life I've contended with the pitying glances of well-meaning people who believe that a show of sympathy is a necessary corollary to my choice.

That doesn't mean that I don't write about children. It just means that I understand (or I hope I do) the resonant power of the literary image of a child, of sons and daughters. After all, poetry is not the making public of one's private diary, even though autobiographical elements will of necessity creep into one's work, much the way pollen creeps into my house in spring, making me aware of its inevitable and essential existence.

And so here, there are two journeys. First, a mother recounts her journey from youth to old age in a symbolic gifting to her son. The second journey is that of the son who has moved away from his childhood home, thereby transforming the relationship into one of memory, on the one hand, and a yearning, on the other. The circular completion of the son's physical journey is mirrored in the emotional completion of the mother's journey. And yes, this is poetry, this is fiction, and this is life.

Jewels

I gave my son a pearl
when I was still young,
when his hand in mine
was like a wild bird
that could not yet fly.

I gave my son a garnet
when I was past middle-age,
when my body had thickened
and my hands begun to stiffen.
And it lay in his palm
like a little drop of blood.

I gave my son a sapphire
at a time when
I could no longer walk,
and though I was bent
almost double
I could not place my slippers
on my own two feet.

My son has left my warm house
and gone off to seek his fortune.
I look out over the water
and wait for the prow of his boat
to round the bend in the river.
And now I think I can see my son
rowing towards the mossy bank,
his oars churning the water
into diamonds.

I am afraid of hospitals, their long, labyrinthine corridors and their odour of sterility.
Yet, curiously (for a healthy former gymnast and current dancer), as I look back over
my work, I see that I've written several poems about illness, infirmity, and disability.
This piece, almost entirely fictional, is based on 'going under' and 'coming round'
from an anaesthetic during a medical operation. The sensation is akin to that of an
astronaut floating in the gravity-deprived atmosphere of the moon, but at all times
there is the comforting sense of another, a loved one, someone who appears to be the
touchstone of the narrator's existence.

Anaesthesia

Down the middle of the moon I cruised,
half of me alight and that sweet taste –
or was it tingle? – of finding a shore of shade

under the second-to-last crater
I came upon. But all too soon

a large breath that I took to tell you of this
lifted me up to starlight height
and I found my tongue glued in a forest of dust,

my body strapped to the bed like a humming-
bird trapped in a wire fence,
trying to regain my senses since the breath
leapt momentarily beyond arm's length
and kicked for touch. Never have I known

a shore-shaped hardened artery
pump so blissfully. You slept like a baby

while the men chopped a deep road into my chest
between my light side and my dark side,
lifted me in silence to the moon and beyond.

☐

And finally, a self-help poem offering both fantasy and advice:

Instructions for Changing Your Life.

I
Start with this exercise for handling
each separate strand of the rainbow:
Look for a spot of violet splashed

on the grass. Pick it up;
perhaps hang it as a wind chime.

Orange is that last argument
you had with your significant other
(yes, you know who I mean).
Erase it.

The red is easy.
It makes a box on the gatepost,
full of sound. You can't miss it.

Blue is insubstantial
and can be found
only as a residue in a small glass bottle
on a shelf by the window.
Any window will do.

Green is that thing clamping
its hand on your wrinkles or liver spots
so you can't wash them away.
Accept them when they arrive. They're yours.

Indigo is the colour of an embrace.
It can be sweet, soppy, challenging, surprising.
You may take as much of this as you like.

 II

The sea does not bleed into the shore,
no, it absolutely does not.
All you need do is fold up
its edges, being extremely careful
not to let any of the water slop out.
Make sure that the salt doesn't leave stains.
There's no need to weigh it.
Now carry this, whether lake, sea, or ocean,
to the small child waiting for you;
the one who's only four. She will ask
if she can hold it for a while.
She says she will be terribly careful.
She will not break anything.
She says she really only wants to look at it
and will return it.
And you say --------.

AHMED PATEL

Ahmed Patel is received gratefully to the quiet of Collingwood St, for the interview. He's tall and slender and speaks with a Johannesburg 'good school' accent. The first part of the exchange is about the Patel family, perhaps better named 'clan', mainly because, as a result of some previous journalism, I became fascinated by these 'vlugtelinge' from Indian poverty in the early Twentieth Century; a group that has become, very quietly and modestly, hugely successful in SA.

But Ahmed's family fortunes didn't immediately change. Ahmed tells me, 'My dad's upbringing was extremely poor. My granddad was a merchant of clothing, he made belts, he'd get buckles and assemble the belts; but before that, he'd sew up work trousers and skirts and sell them wholesale. My grandmother would often work on the sewing machine for hours on end and they'd barely eke out a living for twelve children. This was in Johannesburg, on the West Rand, they grew up in Roodepoort.'

'Where did the family come from in India,' I ask?

'I don't have . . . I guess that's one of my shortcomings when it comes to my personal life, I don't have exact dates and things. I know that my granddad was the first generation; he came here quite young, he was probably in his late teens and he's now eighty. He's still alive, but I doubt if I can extract any information from him. If I ask around among my dad's siblings they may have records.'

I ask again where the family came from in India.

'Yes, from Gujarat, but Gujarat's a big province. I'm not too sure exactly where, I'm so ignorant about my history.'

I say, 'I think you would get to a point in your life where it [family history] would be more significant and more interesting and at that point, everybody will be dead and you'll be tearing your hair out, because you didn't ask any questions.' [Laughter] Ahmed continues, 'You know the thing is, it's not as though my grandparents spoke really fondly of India. They hardly went back. My grandfather has been, probably twice, to deal with inheritance matters. The last time was two or three years ago and he was quite frail. He was accompanied by some aunts and uncles so they would be able to tell me what village he came from.'

I comment that each generation has become more successful, better educated.

'I think that my grandmother, my dad's mom's biggest drive, was education. Although she wasn't schooled, she was always reading and stressing the importance of education. My dad went on to become a teacher for many years and he became quite a senior educator. My uncles were mostly businessmen and my aunts married, it being quite a conservative Muslim Indian family, but a few of my aunts are also teachers.'

'What path did you take?'

'Well, education was always emphasized, but I think I had a little more leeway in terms of what I wanted, I had the luxury of choosing what I wanted to do. Which high school I wanted to go to, which courses I wanted to take at varsity, so I guess that hard work did pay off, to give me that luxury today of choosing a profession. A lot of my cousins didn't get to choose a profession. They were very good at school, but pressured into doing medicine or accountancy or law. You know, those hard professional courses. I chose to do a Bachelor of Arts, and then postgraduate in media studies. I focused on representation through Discourse Analysis.'

I look very blank. 'What is Discourse Analysis?'

[Laughter by both]

'I guess it's a qualitative analysis on how perception is created through different elements in language. How they get broken up to try to convey some kind of message within a particular frame. If you like, that's where the representation comes in.'

I ask whether the Discourse Analysis he's studied has had an effect on his poetry.

'I think so, firstly, though, I always find it hard to consider what I write, as poetry. Because in my mind, poetry is rhyme and you know, it's poetic. Whereas I find the stuff that I've been writing and peddling is very literal. It's not balanced and there's hardly any rhyme and if there is, it's coincidental. I don't think it's poetry, poetry in the sense of what I think "poetry" is. It's more a literal account of things.'

I tell him that I perceive his poetry as quite paradoxical. 'You can be leading me along in one direction and suddenly I'm facing east!'

Ahmed laughs and says, 'That's what I like, that's the playful element, telling a story, almost like a one-liner, the aim of it I guess, if there is an underlying aim, is that it could be funny. I'm criticized for being a very cynical person.'

I respond, 'The cynicism comes through, and the negativity comes through but why I used the word paradoxical earlier, is because suddenly you'll 'about face', suddenly you'll take a different tack, suddenly the negative will become positive. I found it difficult to understand but stimulating.'

westerpark

scarred by annoyance
rooted in fear
     setting off
in a nowhere zone
semi-wonderland
     somewhat sweet

I ask Ahmed how he came to poetry.

'I write a lot about daily accounts, I keep a logbook. I write about events, things that I think are events that I need to report on. It's not structured and it always takes on the same sort of themes in terms of what I don't have and what I would like to have. And that became very mundane, like a kind of a diary of death. Often I think of them [the poems] as doodles while I'm involved in documenting these very routine activities, like taking minutes at a meeting. And while you're taking the minutes you're doodling a man getting stabbed in the back.'

'Do you draw pictures?'

'No, no, no, these things you call poems, those are the doodles!'

'This is your indirect poetic life?'

'Yes [laughs] but I can never imagine them being taken seriously. These mundane things that I take seriously are not really serious. That's why I find it so funny, because I'd imagine they would come off as very serious, readers would take them seriously.'

I get on to the issue of publishing.

'I wouldn't say a lot. The first collection of twenty-four poems, I compiled myself. I had this friend who is a graphic designer, she put together this little booklet for me. I still have that, I think I might have printed one copy for the record.'

'Who reads your poetry?'

'I think the first time I've had my poetry read, that is, quote unquote, "poetry", I'm going to insist on that because I'm still coming to terms with what poetry is, was in an online publication called *Itch*. This was probably five years ago. I contributed to that for a few quarters, whenever they called for submissions, and then I stopped. Then I had another collection of stuff I did with two friends of mine in Cape Town. I think these collections signify different periods as well. And then the last batch of stuff I've had read, well, that was the stuff I read out at the Melville Poetry Festival in 2011.'

I ask whether Ahmed could walk away from poetry, abandon it, get on with his life and never give it another thought.

'I don't think so, because like I said, I like documenting these things and it's not only with writing. I find having a phone these days to be quite like having a Swiss Army knife. You know, it's got all these handy applications. So I'm always taking pictures or videoing things or recording sound clips for documentation's sake. It all kind of fits in, in the sense that as long as I have this notebook with me, I'll have some paper to waste and I will write something on it.'

'Doesn't this constant 'recording' mark the intense curiosity of the journalist?'

'I don't consider myself as a journalist in a public sense. The journalism I do on a practical level is copy editing. I hardly write anything that gets published in a mainstream newspaper. I have but I find I can't keep it up, it's a very curious way of writing. I think the news editing process is much more interesting.'

A brief dialogue

And… what did you say?
     Not much.
Hm.
     What should I have said?
Not much.
     What if I told the truth?
That would be refreshing.
     Hm.
Maybe your truth isn't much.

Ahmed asks what is my intention in allowing respondents to edit their own texts. Then we become involved in an exchange about editing, about the many ways to change meaning, about presenting oneself in the best light if allowed to edit one's own text. It's not an aspect of writing I've ever paid any special attention to, but editing is clearly an important technical and intellectual discipline for Ahmed, stemming probably from his tertiary education and work experience. I express the hope that Ahmed will not turn the text upside down when he receives the transcript for editing, that he will accept his words and 'won't change them inordinately'. But that's not good enough for Ahmed!

'Yes, I don't think there's anything like an inordinate change, any change is significant change, even if it's putting a comma in a certain place. There are many ways to change meaning and it might not even be subtle. It might go unnoticed, but it needn't be subtle.'

We continue and I realize that I'm somewhat at sea, not really understanding his intellectual framework for, and practical experiences with, editing. He tells me that at present (January/February 2013) he's part of a team editing the National Treasury report on government expenditure and that he has to observe specific parameters.

I ask Ahmed when it was he showed a feeling for words and poetry.

'From early high school,' he replies, 'or maybe even before that. I can't put an exact age to it. I've always wanted to jot things down and to note things. I suppose that started when I learned writing and reading.'

'Was there anyone in the family who influenced you towards writing, anybody who played a particularly strong role?'

'I think my dad's brother influenced me. He used to be the imam of the Queen St Mosque in Pretoria. He was very well educated in an Islamic sense but he was not that orthodox, in that he was politically minded and intellectual, even though he'd had the Islamic training. I'd say anti-apartheid but also anti-West, anti-Capitalist. And I think I got a lot of little knick-knacks from him. I'd overhear his debates and discussions with my dad when we went over to visit him in Pretoria. He was a very intense and intelligent man. He was diagnosed with bi-polar disorder when he was fairly young but kept it at bay for a long time. He studied a lot, read a lot and also published some books of poetry. He influenced me broadly, I remember discussions and conversations with him but he never handed a book over to me or suggested some kind of reading.'

Somewhat to my surprise, I discover that Ahmed's home language was English, all his education was in English.

'Well, my dad and my mom spoke Gujarati to my grandparents. It was a sort of kitchen Hindi as such, my parents couldn't write or read it. So it was English all the way. We had to do Afrikaans at school so I picked up a little bit of that but I don't really speak it.'

'And where was school?'

'I started at Fordsburg Primary. My mom decided just before my last year at Fordsburg that it wasn't a good school to go to, so I moved over to Saxonwold Primary. That was just for a year and then I started at Parktown Boys' where I finished high school. I think that's where a sense of rebellion was instilled in me.

There was a fairly rigid hierarchical system not only with the teachers but also among the boys. Among the matrics were the prefects and among the prefects were those who excelled at sport, and so on. The hierarchy tried to impose the things you should do and the things you shouldn't do, and how to conduct yourself.

'But in that whole system, that scary hierarchical system, I found ways to get around it. It wasn't rebellious in that I wasn't mooning teachers in the hallway or anything like that. The friends I ended up associating with, we shared a common understanding of this, so we'd comment on it I guess in a snide way and have a good laugh about it.'

'And I guess that sort of developed your, your . . . secret anarchist,' I suggest.

'Yes, we did not entirely see the point of the system but kind of liked it, because you're getting to socialize with these people. If it wasn't for the system that brought you together you wouldn't have met these people and enjoyed time with them.'

resolution, at last

inside there
       anguish
and there
       and there
pick away
           scratch
smooth over with an impatient
         stroke
scratch again
     harder
into the depths
        of this shallow
   anguish

But Ahmed admits that being part of a close subgroup at an all boys' school didn't ideally develop his social skills. 'That did add a lot to my shyness, but at times I'm not shy. No, it's not a shyness towards people it's more this kind of immediate judgement when you meet someone. You either know whether you're going to try and further some kind of interaction with them in future, or not.'

After a smoke break, looking down upon Bez Valley and across to Observatory Koppie, we continue, when I ask Ahmed if there's anything specific he'd like to say about his poetic life.

'A very important thing to me is time consciousness, in a literal sense. If I arrange to meet someone at 2.30pm, I'll be there. I think that's quite important to me. How it influences what I write . . . it definitely influences what I do, because it has a physical impact on your behavior. But I don't quite know how it influences how I write. Time is important to me. I don't know whether it's time management or knowing how much time I have to do things. I like to prepare. It's mental preparation: what do I expect and what might be expected of me. I am sure I could find some link but we could go on for another hour without coming to any conclusion. So I guess I'll leave it at that.

'Earlier I was thinking when I went outside to have my cigarette, um, as much as I've been stressing on this thing about recording things, keeping records, maybe I've been thinking that the best things are unrecorded. The best images are the ones that you don't take a picture of, and those things that slip through the cracks are what keep you going. Because you think that some day you're going to capture the right image. And if you're doing it often, the chances are you'll capture it. So that's the guiding force, in a sense – that drive to capture a perfect image that's so elusive. In the end you'll get glimpses of it but probably never fully capture it.'

I end this piece with a short narrative section as a result of problems with the final stages of the tape. It would appear that he is a poet becoming, suffering the tribulations that are not unknown to poets generally. He admits to being extremely scared when he read his poetry at the Melville Festival. One thing he "secretly and unrealistically" aspires to is to be a stand-up comedian. He was sorry that his Melville poems didn't elicit more laughter.

□

Moving on

A black wish
    cast as a spell
        whispered
        uttered
            and pollinated
    passed on
    sown
        and spewed
Lands on top of a dead pile
    of hopes and good nature
And settles
    absorbed
    surged
    charged
    and encouraged
        with sneers
        sniggers
        and snorts
It grins then smiles and opens up
        light
        joy
        and happiness

          motherly acceptance
             fawning
             planning
             and motivating
itself

             to be loving
             to be love
                  itself

☐

This was written quite recently. I see it as a kind of climax to an awfully tedious build-up. The few things I wrote in the months preceding this displayed a clusterfuck of ambivalence and perhaps even misplaced affection. A kind of emotional funfair: nothing serious, forced, and not fun (or funny) in the least. I see this as a 'climax' because writing it gave me an exciting little surge, like when a lustful gaze is reacted to favourably. It's some kind of small act of defiance and relative independence. Its sparseness and the fact that I don't dislike it were quite refreshing. Through its jadedness it also presents optimism.

curious intricacy

sliding up and down
this fine, silky thread
to the centre
hanging on
             to catch another
             and another
so many threads
running to the centre
             around the perimeter
the inside layers
          spun so flimsily

☐

LEBOHANG NOVA MASANGO

Nova is pretty, petite and poised and when we meet, dressed entirely in stylish black topped off with a turban. It says, 'I'm different, I'm fashionable.' Confident, with a very clear view of her life's missions, she speaks English with a very slight Anglo American accent. She considers herself a Born Free. I'd like to think the future of the country rests in the hands of young women such as Nova.

By the time Nova reaches me for the interview she and Allan Kolski Horwitz, who collected her from work, have been conversing during a car journey, about her life and life as poet. I suggest she starts off by following some of those themes. She says, 'We had lots of random conversations but one thing I spoke about was the fact that I'm studying anthropology though right now I'm taking a break from that, to do some other things. But the wonderful thing about when I study anthropology [among others, a study of and comparison between different cultures] is that it's influenced a whole lot of my art; so the ability to look at the world theoretically and look at the things that make us different and the things that make us similar and societies and history and contextualize that all into this great wonderful discipline called anthropology, is a lot of what drives me to write the way I do. And my writing is also coming from my history, my parents' history as freedom fighters, which makes me wholesomely passionate about the issues I commit myself to; the issues I deal with in my work.'

'What led you into anthropology?' I ask.

'It came about randomly, because my mother always wanted me to study politics, and international relations and become a diplomat. That was her vision for my life. When I was filling out my course forms I came to the point where there was one left so I chose anthropology. It was a complete accident yet now it has become central, a passion, thankfully you know, like it was just one of those beautiful surprises that life throws at you. I always knew what it was, but I didn't have an interest in it because, *what do you do with this? what kind of work do you do when you have this degree?* But I took it anyway and it was like, *oh my goodness this is what I've been waiting for all my life, now I understand the world I live in, I understand why it is the way it is.* I don't know, maybe I just like talking about things but now I finally have a language with which to articulate how I feel about the world and how the world acts upon me. Yeah, I love anthropology a whole lot.'

I wonder whether her poetry uses anthropological themes.

'I suppose, I suppose, [thoughtfully] there's one poem that I can think of in that regard, *To do list for Africa.* The poem speaks about, like briefly goes into the history of the continent, and with anthropology you learn how, with colonisation, different countries rearranged the education system and deprived people of all that they've known, all their self pride, their culture and just like a mass dispossession happens. *To do list for Africa* is basically saying that in order for Africa to get to a place of collective healing, we have to go back – go back and reclaim and re-collect what was ours. So go back and do that and read the books and listen to the scholars, it's an important thing to do. So I think that's the one poem that was definitely inspired by the fact that I was learning so much about things I hadn't known before. Like all of a sudden I'm sitting in entire semesters that are just African history and it's not like South African history that begins in 1652 with Jan van Riebeeck, it was none of that; this is like what happened in the 16th Century about Mali and different kingdoms and it was just beautiful.'

'Did poetry come before or after anthropology?'

'It came before. I grew up reading. I grew up in Sweden and when we came back to South Africa, I don't remember having that many friends, I don't remember being interested in having friends because my mother had always raised me around books, so my enjoyment of life was centered in my mother and books and that's it. I just grew up reading a whole lot. Mother read to me, we'd sit and read together. Even though I did not know what was happening with the words, I've always had a love for literature. Books are something I associate with love and a sort of maternal nourishment. For me growing up and getting into different kinds of literature and getting into the spoken word – my introduction to the spoken word – it came late, even though I loved writing. It came through Lebo Mashile. She was on TV doing a programme called *Latitude*. I don't remember the year, but I do remember thinking *oh my goodness words can sound so beautiful and they can be written to convey such profound messages,* and I fell in love with the spoken word. So poetry and literature have always been there.'

I ask Nova about the vernacular and what she considers to be her home language.

'English is my home language and I do try my best in other languages as well. Growing up in Sweden where my first language was Svenska. I came to learn English when my mother read to me and when I came here I was very fluent in English. This was in '93 I think. So English has always been the language in which I have been able to communicate best. But I do know other languages and I do speak them, though I haven't had the literal introduction or the literal basis to those other languages whereas with English you think it, you read it, you write it.'

I ask Nova, 'If I were sitting in the audience listening to you recite your poetry, what sort of experience would I have?'

After a tiny hesitation she replies, 'You are experiencing raw, genuine emotions, you're experiencing someone who cares deeply about what she's speaking about, or else, you know she never would have bothered, you're just experiencing all my passion. I mean, poetry keeps me up at night, like getting a line perfect, the way it feels inside me, translating it on the page so that it can feel the way it did to me, so that when you hear it [voice rises in excitement], you're hearing someone who puts a lot into the work, lots of sorrow but also lots of passion and fire, ja.'

'Sorrow for what?'

'Well, some of my poems are sad. Some of my poems are about break ups and boys. And all the political poems I have are sad and angry, so you're hearing lots of anger and in the political ones, even in the personal, there's usually a string of sorrow because that's what actually moves me to write. I can't write when I'm happy.'

I ask whether she writes about the world of women.

'I do write about that, because I'm a feminist. Yet I wouldn't call it Feminist Poetry though my stance on women's issues comes across quite clearly in almost every poem I write. When I'm writing, I'm writing from my position specifically as a middle class, post apartheid young woman, you know, who's navigating this South Africa. I've never personally known it as tumultuously violent but because of my parents' lived experiences, I know that they fought for something and that's not always being realized in the times we live in.'

I mention that I think Nova's word *navigate* is very expressive of the change and confusion that is South Africa.

'Yeah, it's tricky' she responds. 'Life in general is a tricky thing, there are so many things you could always be doing but there's a path, a map to where we want to get to and it's up to you to lead yourself to where you know you should be.'

'Do you harbour ideals for the country?'

'Yes, yes, I do. Oh, my goodness. Well firstly the ANC Women's League has got to go because they are patriarchal and we need a league that is strong for women in this country; that is going to promote feminist ideals because feminist ideals are ideals of love and equality essentially. That's what it boils down to. It's wonderful to be politically savvy and whatever but if you're going to have a good government, you need to have a very strong force of women, always reminding the people in government that women matter and women should not be relegated to the sidelines. Ja, you have to push the agenda of women being a force and of young girls being a force.'

I ask whether she would describe herself as a rapper, a performance poet.

'I think I am a performance poet. My work tends to be lyrical. It's not very dramatic because I don't really sing – I just speak and I hardly use music or other people in the background. It's essentially lyrical, it rhymes and sometimes when I'm delivering it at a fast pace, it could sound like rap but not quite. But I think the aim is to captivate the audience and keep them with me from start to finish and if that means rhyming words, that's fine, as long as they're understood.'

'Do you memorize your poetry or do you read?'

'I memorize it. I am a visible shaker, my paper rattles around when I attempt to read. I notice that I make more sense when I am confident, having memorized, then I can add expressions to it, my hands can move, so it's more freeing for me, having memorized it before.

'I've performed in different venues. I first started in 2011 and that was at 'Word N Sound' at Baseline and then it moved to Emonti Diner on Bree and then we performed at the State Theatre. I've performed on my own at the Joburg Theatre, at UJ [University of Johannesburg], at Wits, also in Cape Town.'

I comment that Nova has taken off fast.

'I try my best to always push the art as far as it can go. My audiences are mixed though mainly young people, university students. I realize that I have an advantage of being around people of my age who regard me as being cool, whatever, so the cool thing about that and knowing that, is that I can be like *hey, guys, books are cool, and*

poetry is cool. And it's cool going to the club because I love going to the club. Saturday
morning you get ready to give a poetry session. I know lots of people my age who just
don't like reading and I can say, do you know how wonderful books are?'

I comment that she perhaps sees herself an apostle. She likes that. Then I ask her
about the future she sees for herself.

'I'd really like to become a Professor of Anthropology, to get the highest
qualification I can, whether here or like at the University of Chicago, or where
ever, but then to come back here and really influence whoever I can influence in
Government in order to get a strong woman's force going. And obviously strong
women's forces do not relegate men, what it is, it's equality, it uplifts everyone. So
that's the one thing I'd really like to do. And with poetry, I'd love to become an
author, a poet, like all of those people who are trusted in the literary world. I'd like
to be trusted, asked my opinion on various things [much laughter here]. I just wish
to become one of those core people recognized and known and loved for poetry and
prose and academic work. With anthropology I love writing essays, I love it. I want
to, wherever my work can go, to spread my message, whatever it is I'm spreading.
My love for anthropology and poetry and my passion for women's equality can all be
done at the same time, everything could link and become part of this mission that
I'm on.'

'Could you live without poetry?'

'No, no, I could not, because then all I have left is hip-hop and that is terrible, that
is terrible, I couldn't do it [laughs]. Poetry provides a necessary balance. All the time
when I've had emotions and depression and things that I couldn't articulate, there've
been songs that I've been feeling and paintings that fuse what I'm feeling, but poets
have a way of just saying it, of articulating me exactly, like you're listening to yourself
in their words. And ever since a poet did that to me for the first time, I decided *that's*
what I'm going to do! I have these tattoos on my body and all of them are poetry
lines, because that's how important this poetry thing is to me.'

'Who are your favourite poets?'

'Whoo, I love them all! The poet who is a fire that I look up to is Sunni Patterson,
I love Saul Williams, I love Stacey-Ann Chin, I love Alice Walker, I love Audre Lord
and Lebo Mashile and Safia Elhillo.'

I confess to not knowing any of the poets Nova has mentioned apart from Alice
Walker.

'Hmm,' she says, obviously not too impressed. I ask whether they are American
apart from the Africans.

'Yes, mostly 'from that side'. Most of them are very new, come to light in the last
ten years, very post modern.'

I play one of my wrapping up questions. 'If you were driving away from here,
what would you regret not having said?'

'Mmm . . . it would be that South Africans have so many untold stories and
unfortunately because of socio-economics, we have the situation where reading
and writing is a privilege and that is so unfortunate because there are stories out
there, not just stories that make you feel warm and fuzzy inside, but there are people
out there who are dealing with some real hardships and it's so sad that poetry and

literature is inaccessible to many. That's the one thing I'd love for us to change, for reading to become a culture. More than literacy, reading to become a culture. Because of anthropology, I understand American cultural imperialism, and that the hearts and minds of the youth have been captured by an influx of American culture. I love rap and hip hop, I love the movies, I love it, I do, but it's so sad that so many people get caught up in that being the only kind of dream that they have for themselves even though it's completely unobtainable in South Africa; you can't live an American dream, it's just impossible. But many do try and it's crazy because there are treasures being lost every day, because there's that person who could have been the most amazing poet but now she's just caught in a web of intangible, materialistic aspirations. So I think that a reading culture in South Africa is essential because that's the kind of thing that widens the scope for people's aspirations.'

I ask about Dad's influence.

'Well, my dad's always been around, my mom and dad have always been together. My dad used to write my mom letters when she was in Russia and he was in Sweden and the UK. He always tells me that *you got your love of poetry from me because I'm a writer.* And it's so weird because she says I got it from her and he says I got it from him. I really don't know anymore, but I do know that my mom was the one who read to me mostly.'

I suggest that Nova grew up in a culture of words.

'Yes, I think so, and we had a massive bookshelf in our house and my mom tells me that when I was two I sat under the bookshelf and played there the whole day. So I've always been fascinated by books rather than dolls or toys. I'd rather be inside with books. For most of my life I've always found, I've found huge solitude in books. I've always preferred books.'

'How do poems come to you?'

'I have to be in a sad place to write, only a sad place. I don't recall being happy and writing. When you're happy, you're so caught up in other things, in celebration and being happy and being, whoo, let's dress up and go to dinner, you know. And when you're sad you are by yourself, you are crying, when I'm sad I'm crying, the lights are turned off and I'm like *oh my God this is the worst feeling in the world.* And from then on it becomes important to document that. For me, writing has always been a purging, a cleansing, so yes, I would call it therapeutic. When we're having those introspective navel-gazing moments, we all think our pain is the worst pain in the world, right? When I'm having those moments and I need to get out of it, I know that I'm going to write. And I tell myself *okay, this is how you feel right now but you are going to write about it and when you have done writing, you are going to turn all of this pain into something beautiful.* So that's how I pressure myself. It's not a conscious thing but a process that happens behind the process. What is left on the page must be beautiful and when you're done with this, every time you feel like this again you'll remember that you wrote something and that something was good, so we can kind of move on. In that way I don't fall into the same depression all the time, I fall into a lesser depression.

'The personal poetry that I write about my relationships is obviously coming from a very real moment of two people falling into the cracks, things getting messed up, so that comes very obviously from me. But the political things that I write – sometimes you come across a story in the newspaper that will break your heart so for the rest of the day you're stuck with that pain. Yesterday I read about Anene Booysens. She's the young girl who was raped and disfigured and her body was thrown somewhere, but before she died, she managed to identify her attackers. And I read today that they've granted her attackers bail and I really cried right there and then. What sort of world do we live in, what sort of South Africa do we live in, where we don't protect women? Things like that break my heart every single day. We've got the Reeva Steenkamp and Oscar Pistorius thing. Everyone knows he killed her but then he goes free and it's like, do we really love the women in our country, do we hold their lives as high as we're supposed to? Knowing that something could happen to you the next day and there'll probably be no justice for your family because this country's justice system just doesn't have time for that.'

Nova agrees with my comment that she's tuned into the world's sadness and from that arises her creativity.

'Anthropology made the world make sense for me. It allowed me to understand the generational oppression of black people, of women, and I'm understanding this from my very own corner of the world, as a black person, as a woman, and I understand how these systems of oppression were set in place over the centuries. It gives you peace to understand how it happened, but then moving forward, you see how it continues to be enforced by the very people who should not be implementing and enforcing it.'

I ask whether she would perceive South Africa as tragic country.

'Yes, we are, but at the same time that slogan *alive with possibilities* is the truth. People are doing amazing things every day, for themselves and for each other. You can't help be inspired every day. So it's cool but it's like we've got all this rot, this festering rot underneath and a few layers of wonderful things. It's like manure and roses, you have to push beyond the shit in order to be awesome.'

Has she published a volume of poetry?

'No, the word is not 'reluctant', the word is that I really like to take my time with things. I feel like there will come a time, I never look for these things, if they come to me they do, but right now I'm just taking my time. It will come within the next few years.'

And earning her bread?

'I do marketing at MTV. I'm part of those people who sell a certain culture to the youth and the saving grace is that I can see how media disseminates to and influences young people. It's very interesting because with my overall perspective, when I do get back to anthropology [I go back to school next year] I'll probably have more insight into capitalism and consumerism. How it determines who gets paid for what, the fact that poets and writers are not earning well whereas executives in America ride around in fifteen sports cars even though they're selling content which is not as valuable as education. It's completely mixed up, but it's interesting to understand the science behind all of this stuff.

'In the world of poetry, and I'm speaking specifically about this new scene of poetry coming out, people of my generation, like my peers, whatever, we slam in Newtown, the spoken word poetry. There is an interesting perception, but I suppose it's changing every day, that you have to be a certain race to be a poet. You have to have an Afro or dreadlocks, you basically have to wear a long skirt if you're a girl, you have to basically look like a rapper and that qualifies you to be a poet, because then people can see that you're coming with a political message that is worth being listened to. And for a very long time that was the perception to the point when I appeared, and you know how I look, which is not that way, people always asked me, *are you in the right place, are you sure you're not lost?* Because I come there with my gear, in my high heels and make-up and people would be like *you definitely don't belong here!* The unfortunate thing with this is that you shun people. It's wonderful to be protective over your art and to maintain standards but it's so important to also be inclusive, willing to hear everyone. When I was in Cape Town I got to hear a young man who was gay, speaking about his experiences. And you don't find that here in Joburg. Not at all! Because here in Jo'burg there's a mentality among the younger poets that you have to be a certain kind of person to deliver poetry. But it's so much better when everyone comes with their stories, when we're listening to everyone and we're taking it in because in that way, we're growing, we're breaking down walls and you're building up something beautiful. So that's the thing in poetry that annoys me a lot, because if I had low self esteem and if I'd taken what those people said to heart, then I wouldn't be practicing something I'm so passionate about even if I do wear high heels and lipstick, It's something that I love so much. Just imagine if their negative voices had shut me up. I think the younger generation should be more inclusive. People should be less afraid to step to the mike.

'My statement of poetics, the reason I do what I do, has always been for what other poets have done for me. That is, they've saved my life on more than one count. My life has been saved by poetry. And what I notice is the common strength around that poetry; those poets have healed me, they have taught me. So my act of homage to those who came before me, to those who saved me, is that I am going to try my best to teach and to heal. That's the one thing that keeps me on track, why I get on stage, because I respect people, I respect an audience. The fact that someone gave up their time, their energy and offered their money to sit there and provide my art with attention. So if I can leave someone with something they can take home, that can play in their minds for the next week, then I'm happy, because if I can add to someone else's feelings or knowledge or something, then I've done my job as an artist.'

I ask whether Nova receives feedback.

'I do. Some of my work is on social networks, on YouTube and Facebook. And this is so amazing, because it sometimes feels like my work has formed a sorority of young women who identify with the messages and it's like, you know what, Nova, I'm going through a bad patch in my relationship and your work has been such an affirmation for me. I feel better and thank you so much. I get messages like that almost daily. That's so beautiful and that's what keeps me going because I'm often too tired or too sad to write. But the fact that there are young girls out there whose lives are a little bit lighter because of what I wrote, that is so satisfying. I have a friend who has one of my lines tattooed on her body and I have so many lines tattooed on my body, it's a sorority.'

I smile. 'So you're a walking poetry book!'

□

This poem was written a few days after the end of one of my romantic relationships. In the very human struggle of coming to terms with pain, anguish and disbelief – beautiful things can be born. That's one of the things that make me grateful to have been born an artist.

Poetry - A Love Supreme: A Lesson in Poetry Women and Jazz Men
(After Coltrane. For M.M)

The night I laid eyes on you is the night I laid eyes on Jazz
All the style and grace I possessed
Held together by Jean Paul Gaultier-Madame
Pink lipstick
Chardonnay and Dunhill Light cigarettes
A Friday night kind of composure
I could tell you were impressed

When I met him
His presence spoke in tongues to my skin
It was written
Everything that is beautiful
Has its beginning in Spring

You a man of music, moving
You, my favourite Coltrane ballad, soothing
Enjoyed you like a Miles Davis chorus
The very first time I saw you
Undeniably
Your fragrance
Captivated me
Like Dizzy Gillespie melody
How light notes of cypress, citrus and violet swirled all around me
How piquant heaviness of Gucci teased me
Closer to conversation
How inside wanted out
I only pretended to be interested in your words
So that I could breathe you in
And land on your mouth

And I did
Again and again
Until, eventually
I knew nights soaked in kisses and drenched in Jazz
By first name

And yet, there would still be so much more to say
About these poetry women and their Jazz men

Lover
Your body became a bebop of endless summer
Swirling cigarette smoke and double-bass lines
Is how we created our own beat
Your tongue traveled down
The burning brown
Brass instrument of my body
Finger tips, felt me
Strong grip, held me
We were a Jazz tune
Kisses overflowed like water
Filled me
Before this
I had spent an entire lifetime being thirsty

In praise of a union this holy
We made music out of movement
The rising sound of gasps and moans
Met the smile of midnight's glow
Like the crescendo of Coltrane's saxophone
We were a Jazz tune

Sexual syncopation
Black bodies like frantic music notation
Spread all over sheets
And I became part origami
Had you so deep inside me
Loved me up! till I felt
Melodies and
Constellations burst in my belly
Proved that heaven
Does not only exist in theory
This is how we loved
And I prayed at the temple of your body
But someone should have warned me
Someone should caution these poetry women

Against these Jazz men
How all we ever do is welcome them in
We find the late nights
Whisky-breath
And sex
Too enticing
Tell me:
How will you ever know which song to sing
When the man you love becomes a metronome?
Which, is to say, a pendulum?
His absence controls you like clockwork
Comes and goes by the hour
Casts long shadows over your adoration
Uncertain of how to hold your affection
You will wonder which prettier, more lady-like version
Of you has now laid claim to him

He will whisper lullabies to your sensibilities
While he hums new hymns into the tongues of other hers
Everything about him will slip through your praying fingers
Trust me
These Jazz men know nothing of stagnation
What do you think they mean when they talk of "experimentation?"
They are in constant search of everything new
Reinvention
They do not believe in single harmonies
These duets never last for an eternity
After they play you
They will pack up every note, rip the chords of your love clean
And then leave you
For the very next interlude
A prettier, more lady-like, version of you
Certainly someone who
Will not wear her heart on her sleeve
By telling all her business on these (Word n Sound) streets
That is the truth, poetry women, about these Jazz men

Yes, your love rose at the beginning of Spring
But soon everything must come to an end
It will be worst kind of Fall
The void he leaves
Will taste like Autumn
Sound like May
Look like leaves clutching their broken hearts
In a death leap for a man who will not stay

Some things just aren't meant to survive the seasons
Some Jazz tunes are just too improv, too beautiful,
Too classic to be repeated

We have no choice but to cherish this memory
But still, I talk us up to God, incessantly
We are Her favourite vinyl record
Plays our Blues by heaven's fireplace
Each night
I weave these pleas out of poems
In hope that it might
Return you to me
But while I have been on my own
I have rediscovered
That there is laughter in living
And ministry in misery
Divinity in dreaming
And prayer in poetry

We will always be a perfect, sun-soaked
Johannesburg love story
Because this is how it must be
When we poetry women fall in love with these Jazz men
A love supreme
Only, never to be played again
A love supreme
Only, never to be heard again
A love supreme

□

This poem was written for an August 2011 performance for Amnesty Wits. It was written as a love letter to this beautiful continent, one of affirmation and healing. I also needed to write a dedication that was not a cliché or a romanticisation of the landscape and human beings found here. I just needed it to be honest.

To-do List for Africa:

When you no longer hate who you are
And the circumstances that brought you here
Undress yourself
Reclaim your weathered body without fear
Stand naked at your Nile
And hold your reflection dear
Behold a brilliance

You, cracked riverbed
Rainforest
Desert
Monsoon
Savannah
Swamp
Almighty harmattan
Spectacle of sand dunes,

Are the wonder of the earth
Cleanse yourself
Bathe in still waters
And while contemplating your future
Flick the chip off your shoulder
Treat yourself to a make-over

Dress in all your splendour
Just like the days of old
Adorn yourself in the armour
Of oil, diamonds and gold

Destroy the robe of martyr
Once and for all

Deprive the stain of colonialism
Any relevance or meaning
Pack your throat full of a narrative
That truly believes in healing

Let it be your song

Sung through centuries
Decades
Eras
And echoed by possibility
Echoed by possibility
Echoed by possibility

See, the sun will forever speak highly of me
Take the sandstorm of my skin as testament
To the survival of Timbuktu manuscripts
And the creations of Egyptian architects
Our blood carries the staying power of ancients
How solar rays cast exact shadows
Was our version of quarter-to-nine

So fuck "African timing"
We exist in a time before time
The sun is our culture

Take this to-do list as a lesson
And, once again, let love be our nature

Africa
I am begging with all of my brownness
Unlearn the word 'pirate'
When speaking of poor Somali people
Actively controlling the destiny of their seas
Against the ever-pillaging, long-arm of European greed
They are protectors

Unlearn the wrath of fire
The way hatred burns down shacks in Khayelitsha
Beats down bodies in Diepsloot and rapes in Alexandra
Leaves the devastation of desperation in its wake
Poor against poor and nothing is being done by the state
Never forget: Harambe

Unlearn your blemishes
Unlearn Idi Amin
Mobutu
Bashir
Mengistu

Unlearn civil war
Coups
Blood diamonds
Kleptocracies
Xenophobia
Genocide
Child soldiers
And casualties

Unlearn your ugly

Africa
My love for you is a broken mirror
Sits heavy in the cavity of my chest
Among dusty boxes full of Fela Kuti songs
And a history bloodied by regret
When I think of you

My heart knows no rest
It skips off track
But once a mirror is shattered there's no way to put back
The pieces
And pieces of turmoil, disasters and diseases
A whole continent of people
Who have been overlooked by the mercy of Jesus
I'm going to need us to love ourselves
A whole lot louder
Even if the 'first' world can't see us

Hold this love up high
Let the splinters of imperfection
Tell the story of you and I
And even if it cuts to tell the truth
Africa
I promise to stop throwing your name around
Like an old excuse

So, remember
When you no longer hate who you are
And the circumstances that brought you here

Undress yourself
Reclaim your weathered body without fear
Stand naked at your Nile
And hold your reflection dear

☐

Re-Enacting October was written as a reminder to accept and to let go, which is often one of the hardest lessons that life repeatedly teaches us.

Re-Enacting October

The moon is in awe of how we rose
Like morning at night
Against a sky that we don't own

In the glisten of your sweat
The Joburg of that night
I experience the seduction of Jean Paul Gaultier – Le Male
Fragrant bursts of orange blossom
Amber

Sandalwood
Cinnamon
And lavender
Play hide-and-seek all across your skin
And I would die
A thousand times
Just to breathe you in
Just to be born again
Because when moments like this begin
Your body becomes religion
And I not having all of you
Is tantamount to sin

Again, the story unfolds
A lover and another one of those . . .
So I proceed to limb-for-limb wrap myself around you
In nostalgia
Keep you prisoner to the heat of this moment
More hope than hell
We cast a spell
Of laughter rising from hips
Meant to have you heaven-bound
And bound to my bed
Hushed the voice in my head
Telling me you would return to her instead

Re-enacting October
Your body feels like dancing
But that night
It hurt like leaving
And even in the sometimes of wrong against right
I still want to experience your rhythm
Want to love you like I love Hip Hop
The way I hold Jazz to my belly
And balance Blues on the tip of my tongue
Want to adore you clavicle-kisses
Skin strokes of blue notes
And percussion in lower back
I want to cherish you
Heavy
And whole
Hold me
Like secret

But, my heart is too keen
These arms, they linger open too long
The moon is in awe of how we rose
Like morning at night
Against a sky we don't own

So, this is to lay mistakes and memories to rest
Months of misunderstanding were resolved
By kisses like night prayers
A cacophony of questions caught in caress
And quietened into a hymn on skin
Truth is
I don't want it to happen again
Trying to find a goodbye – and mean it
Maybe I should walk away – so you can see it
Let it all go – and this time we should believe it
Because I remain in all this misery – and you can't even feel it

More sadness than soil
Holding on to hope and thin air is hurting
This back and forth has me salt-pillar and crumbling
I don't want you in parts and pieces
The possibility of broken-hearted
Is now too close to home
This picture is all wrong
Because I'm all alone
And you're either going or gone
And, I am growing tired of Re-enacting October
It brings me no kind of joy to admit it,
But, Nova
Sometimes you are nothing like your mother's daughter
You only flirt with danger to regain some lost sense of power
Men, who are never yours to keep
You pack too much heat in your dainty ballerina body
For them to know any kind of rest
You haunt them in their sleep

Yet again,
You are the same mistake
That every man in your bloodline has ever made.
You have given face to the shame
Felt by your mother
Your grandmother
And every great, great . . .
For whom the sound of a man's footsteps

And a shutting door are commonplace
They are turning in their graves

You are that Black Magic Woman
Who laid claim to their present
And ripped their futures apart
There is no way to get past this
You curse your own heart
Lonely girl,

You throw your love at men like broken bottles
As if the only way to feel is to be cut first
You welcome the bruises
You thrive off the hurt
Until hands and heart begin to haemorrhage
Into this open wound that you
Find glory in writing poems with
Lonely girl,
Stop throwing your love at men like broken bottles

As if drawing blood will be the only lasting proof of this
The only lasting proof of us
The only lasting truth of this is:
Being the other woman means you will always be left behind
When he finally realizes what's right
Inevitably

Lover,
I can't see how I'm going to settle into this strange world of not enough
A russssssssh of silence shaped like a Joburg sky-line
Stretching between us
Knowing that somewhere beneath this piece of sky
You're draped in the affection of another woman's touch
More sadness than soil
Truth settles like dust

I can't survive these liberations

This heart is too keen
These arms, they linger open too long
And still
The moon is in awe of how we rose
Like morning at night
Against a sky we don't own

Lionel Murcott

Dear Mike and Cecily,

Thank you for making the trek across from Kensington to be part of our party. It was good having you here.

Mike, I just thought I'd pass on to you that – after all my insistence by letter that folk singing is peripheral to me now – I sang two sets of songs to the gathering on the patio later in the evening. It was agreed I sang very well – though Lionel-the-painter felt rather upstaged by his little brother Lionel-the-folk-singer.

Michael the saxophonist at the last Full Moon evening said to me, If you've been a musician it stays in you. I guess it has, though I try to identify myself as painter and poet . . .

Be well,

Lionel (and Jansie)

I usually carry spare batteries for my tape recorder. Arriving early, sitting in the car outside Lionel Murcott's Blairgowrie house for a few minutes, I discovered: no spares. And guess what? That's the day that those in the recorder packed up. So here we started with lovely material that did not find its way on to the tape. After various frustrations and purchasing new batteries at a nearby supermarket we finally got going – again. Throughout the experience Lionel was the acme of patience and tolerance, but I wondered what he was secretly thinking about my journalistic professionalism!

Lionel is a multi-talented artist, he paints, he writes poetry and songs. He plays the guitar, he sings. He is also one of the most energetic creators I've ever come across. He never seems to stop painting or writing or composing or performing. I asked him whether he found time to eat or sleep. He raised his mug: 'I'm drinking coffee,' he replied. He looks like an artist, with beard, moustache and shoulder length grey hair. Lionel, now retired from teaching at the National School of the Arts, the last of several art teaching posts during his working life, has 'never been so busy'. I walked into a living room filled with art material for a shortly to be held exhibition. Eventually, after the battery hiatus, we got moving again.

He didn't at first intend to follow an artistic career.

'My science teacher in school said to the class, a BA is not worth the paper it's printed on. And I happened to be going out with his daughter [roars of laughter] so I took notice. After matriculating I heard of a job at the fertilizer research unit at

AECI and went and became a lab technician, and discovered I wasn't a scientist. My bosses told me that, towards the end of the year. Protesting I said, well maybe not chemistry, maybe the life sciences? 'We don't think you're a scientist Mr Murcott!'

So Lionel started a BA at Natal University, Pietermaritzburg with English Literature prominent. Halfway through the year he found himself carving a fallen piece of split pole fencing.

'My fingers were itchy to take the centre of gravity elsewhere, away from all the head stuff. And I carved, yes, all sorts of things into that largely abstract hollowing of the wood. I carved all sorts of experiences and feelings into it. It was a live thing.' And that experience caused Lionel to change from a straight BA to a Fine Arts degree.

'I was lucky, I didn't have a huge portfolio, I think I had two drawings and two carvings. And the Professor said, 'You mean History and Appreciation of Art?' I said, 'No, no, no, painting and drawing and carving and stuff.' He said, 'Well, just for one year?' I said, 'Yes.' He ended by saying, 'It's not usual but there's nothing in the book says you can't, all right, you're in.'

'You must have made an impression,' I say, 'those carvings must have been startling?'

'Both of them were given to the family that was sort of my alternate family while I was down there. They were a lovely experience. My parents were quite old when they had me, they were quiet, serious people. And this family, neither of the parents had been settled enough to get matric, but they were highly intelligent and explosive and wild and they had seven children. They never earned enough money to have a settled existence, so they would move from one rented house on the outskirts of town, to another. And I arrived there [laughter] and I'd come home! They were just what I needed. The seven siblings were there. I just fitted into this wild family. And there, I learnt to tell stories.

'I was a very serious student. One evening – Sandy and Doreen for some reason entertained in their bedroom, it was comfortable there – the three of us were sitting there, Sandy was reading a photographic magazine, he was a photographer, and Doreen and I were talking away, nineteen to the dozen. And this five year-old appeared in the doorway, didn't say anything, just crooked her finger. I looked at her and I got up. 'This way, down the passage.' I followed her into her bedroom. She jumped into bed, pulled up the bedclothes and said, 'Now, tell me a story!' I thought, my goodness, I've never told a story in my life. But I gave her an image (which I turned into a poem forty years later). It was about a child, a girl climbing up into a big yellow flower and looking up into the blue sky with the yellow petals all around her. That was all, but she loved it. Every time I went there after that, she or one of the siblings said, 'Story time.' I found, a story is like a piece of string. If you've got one end, and you keep pulling, the rest will come.

'My mother wrote many letters. To relatives especially; to us when we were away from home. They just flowed, not literary, about what was happening round her, about what she noticed. So I grew up where writing was natural and interesting. When I was a student in Pietermaritzburg I wrote back, mostly every week. Once, later on, she said, 'You know, I don't feel the week has properly happened until I've written about it.' 'That's the writer, Mum.' Oh, and she used up every bit of the page – up the side and upside down along the top . . . I guess that's how I compose a drawing – the full page.

'I liked English at school. I got the English subject prize in matric. I had a couple of verse translations of Catullus published in the school magazine – I'd prefer them to be forgotton. But good for me to experience Latin prosody, the formal structure. I read science fiction, Ray Bradbury and HG Wells. Listened to the Beatles and the Stones. I wrote well – but getting it down on paper was hell, I procrastinated and moaned to my mother. I loved Blake and George Herbert and Tennyson, and Hopkins – I recited a poem of his in my matric orals. Years later, when I encountered the west coast of Scotland – I was staying in a crofter's cottage converted to a Youth Hostel, beside a stream – the whole of Inversnaid (except the title) came bit by bit back to me and I recited it aloud in a kind of blown-away burnside delight. Judson Jerome wrote, A written poem is like a musical score, a set of instructions for performers. 'Today I know you also as a painter, when did that artistic specialization surface?'

'It's a sign of a sort of craziness on my part. At the end of my first year Fine Arts I had to decide, am I going to do painting or sculpture? The first year was a mixed course. And I felt pretty confident about sculpture, I felt, I'm in touch, I felt I knew where to go. So I better do painting because I haven't a clue about painting. I don't know how to paint and I don't know much about colour, so I better go for painting, then I'll learn. And ja, I've been painting consistently ever since.'

'Have you spent much time with sculpture?'

'I did for a while, with clay. I made rather wonderful hand coiled vessels and sculptural forms with slabs of clay. When I lost access to a kiln I stopped doing sculpture.'

I suggest that he doesn't miss sculpture much.

'I sometimes think that I would like to again paint on plates or platters, but the painting on canvas and paper and the drawing, are enough. I don't need to go back to clay.'

I mention that Lionel has spent much of his life as an art teacher, most recently at the National School of the Arts [NSA] from which he recently retired.

'I spent just over a decade there.'

Apologising for such a black/white question, I ask him whether his teaching, the need to earn a living, developed or frustrated his artistic talents.

After some consideration Lionel says, 'I think, on the whole, it developed me. For instance, when I got to the NSA, one of the other teachers said to me, 'Oh, I'm dreading this winter, the printmaking is going to wreck my hands.' I said, 'I'll do it for you,' and she quite literally handed over the printmaking department to me, because of the effect it would have on her fingernails and the skin of her hands.

'Now, I had done printmaking under William Kentridge at the Johannesburg Art Foundation but that basically consisted of etching, a little bit of monoprint in black and white, but mostly etching. However, that wasn't enough, I had to teach other stuff, so I taught myself linocuts and woodcuts and colour reductive relief prints. Now printmaking is something I love passionately and a room of prints will feature in this upcoming exhibition.'

'And you love portrait painting as well?'

'Portrait painting is the centre for me. I was greatly encouraged by reading that Van Gogh said the portrait is the highest form of art, because I'd always felt that there were other things that were central and the portrait was a kind of poor relative. And certainly the hierarchy in Van Gogh's time was history painting at the top and portraits and landscapes down near the bottom. And I partly believed Van Gogh. I mean he gave me permission to rate portraits more highly, but I still feel it's not enough to be a portrait painter, one must do more . . . such as groups of figures. But I do know that with portraits I crack it time after time, they give me an enormous amount of pleasure, they are uncanny likenesses, they're not just academic likenesses, they go further. They catch something of the [sitter's] spirit, something of the inside as well as the outside. Ricky Burnett used to say that when you're working from life, the subject is here and you are there and at that meeting point in the middle, the work happens.'

'So you're in it too.' Another thought comes to mind. I ask, 'Would you say that any of your poetry is portraiture?'

'Yes, yes, I had a piece published in *New Contrast*, a couple of years ago. It was in several sections about a friend of mine, Rita Strey, who had died by that stage. I think that's a portrait of Rita, a complex, many-levels portrait.'

'Did you ever make a decision to choose between poetry and art? You've always seemed to combine the two, at least for as long as I've known you?'

He replies, 'When I went to the Art Foundation I thought I'd done with writing and theatre and stuff. And found Lionel Abrahams was giving a writers' workshop for the full-timers – he pulled me back into literature. And it was a totally different kind of literature. I love Hopkins, I love Hughes, I love Shakespeare. What he did was to get us to write out of personal experience. Don't worry about the rest of the stuff, start with a vivid experience and convey it directly, in simple language. And that got me going. I've never stopped. The dual thing has gone on . . . both sides were strengthened by being at the Art Foundation and both have never let up.'

We pass on to the primary, early poetic influences in Lionel's development.

'About other poets and issues like form and content, when I was a student, I studied DH Lawrence. I soaked him up! He was just the most extraordinary . . . he was in a totally different place, I was a puritanical, inhibited young man and Lawrence was not. When I was down in Cape Town as an education student I got hold of his *Look! We Have Come Through!*, literally a verse novel, and read the whole thing – and of course it is intensely personal, a kind of diary of his involvement with Frieda. I read every thing of his that I could get hold of. Lawrence's mature poetry is very much free verse, immediate responses to powerful sensations. So I was writing after him in some of my early poetry. I was using him as an early model. But then I was also crazy about WB Yeats. He's very much more structured and rhythmic. So I then tried writing in a much tighter form like a pentameter line. Lawrence is an immediate talking voice and Yeats is a crafted voice. So I was soaking up those two, I was also taking note of Hopkins and the way he uses sound.

'And I read a lot of Robert Graves. What a lyric poet he could be! Somebody said that Robert Graves' is the only poet whose collected works get shorter and shorter year by year. Every time a new edition came out there was less in it. He would edit ruthlessly, anything which no longer came under his definition of poetry, would go. So an utterly magnificent poem about the First World War was thrown out for not being a love poem. It was slightly Yeatsian, which was also a reason for throwing it out, for he couldn't stand Yeats. Graves was one of those great negators. He pulled down one major figure after another and got satisfaction out of it, as if he was the only one left standing. He wrote off Eliot, Yeats, Auden, Pound, all the major figures. And this is a very bad thing for a young man to read, because I have a tendency to follow someone with his certainties.

'Interestingly enough, Graves had a lot of time for e e cummings. And for Frost, he had the highest regard. Those were the two who made it. Graves was a great influence on me, an influence I had to fight against as well and I was convinced that I had to write in iambic pentameter. And then, I think, Lionel Abrahams loosened that.'

I ask, 'Could we go so far as to suggest that Lionel turned you into your self, turned you into your own poet under his guidance?'

'Yes, mm, yes. I'm more able to look at myself and I'm able to take the experience and put it down. Trust the experience and trust yourself as the conduit of that experience. A key text – just before I went back to university to do English Honours, I borrowed a copy of Brookes and Warren's *Understanding Poetry*. It took me through the evolution, all the way from the scribble on the back of an envelope, of Randall Jarrall's *The Woman at the Washington Zoo*. Poetry as process! I started writing seriously, draft after draft.

'I think that one of the things that confirmed me as a poet was a disastrous love affair I had in my first year at the Art Foundation. It was a mature love affair, I was in my thirties. I got involved with a girl who was deeply damaged, she'd had appalling experiences as a child and they'd marked her. She couldn't really commit and she couldn't really let go. It was dreadful really, looking back, and I wrote about that, that dilemma and her and us and the progression of our involvement. And the fact that I was able to write about it, meant that I could survive it.'

'So poetry was therapy?'

'Yes, I think that was important to me. Though as Bill Ainslie said, 'The best therapy happens when you make the best art'. There was another situation some two or three years later where I had become a close friend of Carl Niehaus.'

'You had a hell of an experience round that!'

'It was . . . you know, to have to go to court and testify against a man who not long before that had been the best man at my wedding. I'd been married less than a year. My life was opening up. I realized that I'd spend the rest of the year in jail waiting for the court case. And then I could have been charged with handing out anti-conscription leaflets, which Carl and I did together. I didn't have the constitution, psychological constitution, that would allow me to go through with something like that really. I would probably crack up. So I was caught in all sorts of . . . and I wrote my way through that, I went on writing for years and years, trying to deal with the guilt and the pain of that. He had a long sentence, high treason. So this therapeutic situation, yes, writing has been a good therapist for me. Yes, that one was tough and the irony is that I'm now married to Jansie, who'd been Carl's partner then and married him in prison. But I write about situations like that, immediate situations like that, and then the spin offs from them – the stories Jansie tells me end up as poems. So I've got a mountain of stuff that is currently unpublishable, too private.'

I refer to Lionel's intense energy level: always painting always writing.

'Yes, I do a lot. I'm currently painting more than I'm writing but there's quite a good body of written work as well. I've got a book coming out on the Web soon. Print is a lot of stuff to chase and I probably won't get anywhere. I've got an eighty-page book called Cupboard Skeleton which will be coming out in a couple of months. I've got to get the hang of working this programme – it's on a blog and the poems just have to be rearranged. It was a big step but I met someone at the Bus Factory in Newtown where I do my prints and he said, 'If you want stuff on the web, I can help you, I'll swop those services for artworks.' Some irony, old fashioned, hand printed woodcuts in exchange for a slot on the web [laughter].'

We move to politics and white disillusion. Lionel says that when he went to vote in the Great Election – 1994 – he wore the ANC colours.

'A black pair of pants a green shirt and a bright yellow tie. That great queue, creeping around the base of the koppie and eventually into the Kensington Hall. It was just such a wonderful day. I had so much hidden loyalty to the ANC and such a tormented history as a result of it. But now that seems to have fallen away. Now I'm sad and skeptical and removed. Jansie is still more involved because she was after all a member all these years. Her membership took her underground and into jail. But she's also conflicted by what she sees.'

I ask whether politics ever directly informed Lionel's writing.

'I've come close to it a couple of times. Recently, I wrote a poem about Archbishop Tutu's comments on the present government. And most closely perhaps, when Charles Bester, this was before the change, was to be tried for conscientious objection. There was a vigil for him at St Paul's in Parkhurst. He was to appear in court the next morning. It was an acknowledgment of him and a kind of 'off you go, my lad'. My then wife and our children were on holiday partly to give me a chance to get into marking. I went home to mark and I marked all the rest of the evening. Then I gave myself a treat, and read aloud a group of Yeats' political poems, "A terrible beauty is born." And then, as I switched off the sitting room light, this voice started up: Charles Bester, conscientious objector – Yeatsian rhythms – and I switched the light on again. For the next couple of hours I wrote about his stand. Early next morning I phoned Nick Paton whom I knew was going to the trial. I said, 'I've got this poem for Charles.' He said, If you can get it to me within the next half-hour. Okay, so I jumped in the car, gave it to him, he passed it to Charles Bester who read it to himself in the dock and then passed it to his dad. And his dad published it in the ECC magazine. And it is quite a directly political poem. But there haven't been many – in fact my long cycle, probably around a thousand lines about the Carl thing, is asserting my right to bear witness to the experience rather than be the engaged one.'

'Would you like to say anything about your song writing?'

'Yes, Yes. When I left school, my Uncle took my cousin and I to a folk concert. It was just the very first breaking in of folk music to the South African scene in 1965. And I was absolutely entranced. I'd performed in Gilbert and Sullivans, I'd sung in a choir, I'd done all sorts of things but this was it for me! So after that I went out and bought a second hand guitar and a book *Teach Yourself Guitar* by Jerry Silverman. My brother and I learnt to play. We learnt folk songs, American and English folk songs. For the next year that took all the time and energy which work did not take, and for the next two years I was a fanatical folk singer. Best training for a someday poet.

'We tried to compose our own songs, appallingly, the group, it didn't work. Later I set some of Graves' poems to music. I wrote some of my best material . . . ha, therapy again, I was in therapy – that bad relationship you probably remember from Kensington. I said to my therapist, 'This person's car on the pavement' – that was the line I used – and she said, 'That sounds like a line out of a country and western song.' I didn't take it as being particularly complimentary but halfway home I stopped and wrote a country and western song. That evening I phoned Roy Blumenthal and sang it to him over the phone. 'What about putting in a bridge,' he said, and had to explain what a bridge was. I put it in, and it worked. Then followed four or five more, in the folk tradition, accompanied by the guitar. They're quite powerful songs, good songs. I dusted them off about ten years later and sang them at a Full Moon event, last year. And I found after that, these songs were going round and round in my head. I said, 'This is ridiculous, these old things in my head about a relationship that was dead long ago. I must write something new.' So crumbs, what the hell and into my head jumped this voice, [sings] 'Edvard Munch, Edvard Munch.' I said, 'That's it.' So I wrote another song. Mind you, I'm just an occasional singer-songwriter. The painting and the poetry demand to be central.

'Munch, yes, he's one of the giants, Munch, Picasso – two really big ones. If it was a good image and still invested with stuff for him, Munch would do it again. He did four versions of *The Scream*, each one subtly but quite different from the others. Yes, I recycle images, definitely. Ooh, of course the other thing about . . . jumping back to Robert Graves, he used to endlessly prune, cut away, edit his poems and I got into this perverse pleasure in doing that. But also you move closer to something that is condensed and powerful. I know that Alan Finlay would like me to sit down and write a poem off, bang, one time. But I never stop editing. Finlay says my paintings are once-off, why can't I do it with poems? But they're different, in fact the differences between the paintings and the poems are fascinating. The poems are more wrought and I think more formal in a way, but the paintings get their unity and their completeness from the physicality of the movement across the canvas or the paper.'

I mention that Allan Kolski Horwitz talks about sculpting a poem.

Lionel replies, 'The word that jumps into my head concerning the reworking process is 'chipping away', and, of course, that is sculptural. Getting the final image, getting all the dross cut away. I find I do lot of that. I don't think there's a poem where I haven't had to do anything. There are some where it's just on and on and on.'

I ask Lionel what it is that determines the variable length of his poems.

'The experience, basically. When I was writing about Rita Strey there was so much. She worked with Abbe Breuil on interpreting and recording Rock Art in Namibia. She talks about a book she wants to write about all the different colours that we have in South Africa and how we're so anguished and different. She had wonderful furniture and objects. She'd say, this wardrobe is probably from the Medici Palace, Italian Renaissance. And then she got rid of them all – said she was being owned by her possessions. Just kept her TV and a decent chair and table. She was one of my wise old women. It's always been important to have a wise old woman in my life. I met her when I was doing English Honours at Pietermaritzburg. She was my great encourager, I always need encouragement. She was marvelous and I kept contact off and on.'

And so we close down. In rounding off, Lionel says, 'The exhibition I've got on at the moment is entirely portraits and figures and situations involving portraits and figures. I deliberately didn't put any landscapes on though I have a few. I also didn't put any abstract work on either. I think the core of my writing is also about people. So when my mother was ailing, I started writing poems about her, poems about her death and poems looking back, and ended up with a collection of about forty poems memorializing her. The same with my father, I was at his bedside for several days as he lay dying and I brought out a little booklet of poems about his journey. So I think that's one of the commonalities between my poetry and my painting: it's relational, it's people, it's encountering people. Yes, it's that.'

□

I'm fascinated by Lucian Freud's paintings and etchings – even though my impulsiveness and impatience (and my tendency to resolve a painting in one session) may seem very different from his obsessive doggedness as he pursues a likeness over many months. But he is no slick photorealist: his paintings and etchings are built in an accretion of distinctive marks.

I love browsing in bookshops. Big art books are usually out of my financial reach – but can be pulled down off a shelf in Exclusives, Hyde Park, and soaked up. This poem was written after such a visit. Freud's etchings, like his paintings, were done from life, the grounded copper plate propped on an easel like a drawing board.

Having chipped away at this piece with almost Freudian patience, I assumed it complete. Last night, readying it for the book, it bothered me: of the sitter no picture, only a mention. So, to visualize it further, I have worded out of the web a face such as Freud might have seen.

HIS MARK II
(after an etching by Lucian Freud)

1

A web.
Line-bodied, a
nose
rounds – lips,
their weight, half-
open – eyes
puzzled,
focus –

every
scratched-in
mark – laid
rank by
file, across
the copper sheet – is a
centre; of this
one touch by
stared-for one
cluster: his
still
sitter.

2

The love
is in
the scrutiny.

□

Friends of ours needed to retreat from the pollution and pressure of Joburg. So, once
they had found a place in a little dorp at the base of a row of hills, they sold their
Melville house. They now had far more space than in a suburb, and a cluster of
buildings on it. One was turned into a spacious guest cottage; we got to stay in it.
Electric storms on the Highveld are to tell of; and particularly with the sky unbleached
by streetlights, and granite hills looming.

NIGHT STORM AT GEMOEDSRUS

out of the night
steep
drops the rain

shushing thudding
dark
on the roof
of the room
dry hollow drum
where the couple lie
bedded

lightning slashes
white
on the curtains

thunder stutters
crumples
and opens

he moves in
her
wet

from high
high the dark
rain winds them in
held
and still

□

I've already dealt with the background to this poem in the body of the interview.

C.O.

Charles Bester, conscientious objector –
his shock of unruly dark hair,
adolescent angular body,
hands thrust into his pockets
to keep them from trembling – stands
before a packed congregation
and speaks of those who have helped him,
speaks of the family who love him,
speaks –his voice overcome
by a knot of tears in his throat –
of his parents;
at a vigil in northern suburbia
on the night before his trial.

In the Advent dark of the chapel
we watch with him. The flame
from the candle of justice (wreathed
in barbed wire) multiplies, with message
on message: Cosatu salutes you;
a Nigerian bishop prays for you;
from Cape Town the Archbishop assures you
that light and truth have the victory;
a mother applauds your refusal
to fire on her sons in the township;
we're reminded: the feast of Hannukkah
affirms the small band of the righteous
hedged about by the strong and the many.

We weep with the tears of a mother.
There is sweat and pain at a birth.

One by one the small candles are lit.
From the night will rise a new day.

□

This one was written shortly after my mother's death in 2003. It's one of forty I wrote
about her as she became more frail, and after her death; I made several drawings,
too. They're rooted, I suppose, in coming to terms with her mortality; and recording
experiences while they were still fresh. And are expressions of love for her. She played
an enormous role in my formation and my life; well, mothers do. In many of the poems,
I'm mourning.

NEVER AGAIN

The last time I saw her she was propped up on pillows,
eyes tight shut; lips, without the false teeth, fallen.
Ninety-six years had worn her body thin,
surprisingly small. Had left their marks,
the swollen knuckles, blotches, the blurring
eyes and slack eardrums. At four a.m.
when she was used to wake, life slipped from her.
Her body lies in an undertaker's fridge –
after the funeral will burn to ash.
I want to know that this is not her end,
that the Light of light Himself has hugged her,
infused the dead flesh with sweet radiance
in the crackle of his own resurrection.
That she is in the communion of saints. And that's

all very well for the believer. But I'll
never again kiss her, stoop to hug
a little gingerly the narrowed shoulders
(in her forget-me-not blue dress. We've boxed up
her clothes for charity already). I'll never
have to repeat a phrase till her ears
decode it – nor get her direct yet gentle answer.

She'll not ask, Is Emilia still painting her face?
At her age I was playing with a ball –
puzzlement, disapproval in her cheeks.
Nor question, Sam and I fallen out,
how Emilia – so fond of her – was taking it.
I keep turning to the phone: again
know there's no connection where she's gone.

☐

*We got a puppy earlier this year, a curly-white cutie. He's not quite a year old,
sweet-natured; but finds the world outside overwhelming . . .*

WALKING POPCORN

At the first lamppost, nose down: Check, check this,
just a few hours dried, some doggy, what hormones,
and what what did he have for breakfast, no,
from a packet? and he chewed a rich high bone . . .
Hey Pops, we came here for a walk.

There's a dog in the park there's a
dog in the park there's – electric leaping-shocks –
there's a dog. Yes Pops. They're allowed,
that's what a park is for. There's a dog,
I play a D on his stretched-tight leash.

There's a man on the pavement there's a
man on the pavement O my dog there's
a man on – Pops, he's allowed to be,
that's what pavements are for, and anyway
he's got a jogger's licence. A man, a man –

Enter: three dogs, collie-size. Dog. Dog.
Two come up: Hello. Pops orbits on his leash,
Scream, teeth-scream, slings at the bigger – until
his collar pops over his head. The stalk. The tackle. Alone
again, I kneel on him, yelling, re-fasten it.

Walking Popcorn?

□

Makhosazana Xaba

Well known poet, Makhosazana [Khosi] Xaba, kindly drives to my house so we can converse quietly as renovations are taking place next door to her home. We have not met formally although we've heard each other read poetry at the recent Melville Poetry Festival. She's somewhat regal in appearance but very friendly and easygoing. She had already, readily agreed to help me with this project. As I moved through the transcript, I became aware of her go-getting personality and her intense enthusiasm for life and involvement in the literary world. I became aware of her drive to become a writer. Her deep and expressive voice held me spellbound. My opening question was: How did you come to poetry? Khosi's response was immediate but the extended answer emerged at several places as the interview unfolded.

'I was part of a writing group that started in December1999. There were five of us and we met once a month on a fixed date in someone's home where we'd also have lunch. We weren't a group of poets, just writers. From the start we agreed we needed a facilitator so we asked Lesley Cowling to come and help us with writing exercises. The idea was to just bring whatever you had written. In time the group suggested I submit the poetry I was writing. But I wasn't calling it poetry and I thought, really, is this really, really poetry? The first 'things' I submitted, were to 'Women in Writing', an organization in Soweto. Thembeka Mbobo picked three of my poems because she was putting together an anthology for women and youth that was published in 2001. That was very exciting. Next, she compiled a calendar which featured a poem per month. She picked one of my poems for that and that was even more exciting.

'I decided then to pay more attention to poetry and I went into bookstores in order to understand who was publishing what. I used to walk into Exclusive Books, go through the volumes of poetry anthologies. That research led me to conclude that Timbila Poetry Project was publishing new voices and many were black. Soon thereafter I was listening to the radio and they were talking about a workshop for writers and publishers to be run at the Market Theatre and I said, okay, let me go there, gate crash and find this Vonani Bila guy. He chose four of the five poems I submitted. They were in the Timbila anthology of 2002.

'Anyhow, when that anthology came out I called him and I said, 'Listen, could I have twenty books. I'm going to a conference in Malaysia and I'll sell them when I'm there. He said. 'Really, you'll sell twenty copies?' I said 'Why not?' I mean, I was very excited, I didn't see why anybody who knew me at the conference wouldn't buy a book. So we arranged and I got the books and I was in the plane and I went to Malaysia and sold all twenty books and I came back and I said, 'Mission accomplished!' It was at that point that he said to me, 'There's been such a good response to your poetry and I believe there's more where that came from. I'd like to publish a book of your work.'

'And then I panicked, because I didn't think that I had that many poems. I went to my computer to systematically find everything on file and everything I ever knew I'd written. I typed everything and was pleasantly surprised to learn that I had just over fifty poems. I thought fine, we can do something with this. So I worked with Vonani and he was happy to publish my book but he didn't have funding, so that's why the book only came out in 2005 even though it was ready by December 2003. That's a summary of how I came into poetry. So when *These Hands* was published it was very exciting for me, it was like WOW, I'm a poet.' [chuckles, laughs]

'Let's go back a bit,' I say. 'It was obviously in you, the talent was there. You went into that writing group, what sort of age were you at that point?'

'I was forty-two.'

'What took you into that group, what was driving you at that point? Did the need to write start earlier?'

'I have wanted to be a writer for as long as I can remember. The very first book that made me think I wanted to be one, this was at the age of eight or nine, was *Jock of the Bushveld* – can you believe it? My father named the family dog 'Jock' and that had come from his love of the book. But I remember reading it as a child and thinking, WOW, I love this story! That book made me want to be a writer. I was very good in primary school, my compositions were selected and read to the class. When I went to high school, the same thing happened. And I really enjoyed writing essays.'

'Were you doing this in English?'

'In primary school it was in isiZulu. In high school we had to do essays in isiZulu, Afrikaans and English. I grew up in Ndaleni next to Richmond, that's the Midlands. So I went to primary school in Ndaleni, I went to secondary school at Pholela High School in Bulwer next to the Drakensburg mountains, then I did my matric at Inanda Seminary. When I left Pholela High School, two of the teachers (of isiZulu and English) each asked if I could leave my composition exercise book with them. Even in matric, my essays were used as model essays. I quite liked this, I really, really did enjoy it and of course I was reading a lot. But after matric it just seemed more important, more urgent, to be in the Struggle, so slowly I became an activist. But because I never stopped reading, I was learning about writing, perhaps learning is too strong a word, but I never stopped reading. Even when I didn't pursue writing actively, I was reading.'

I interject, 'You were keeping the word alive!'

'Exactly,' says Khosi. 'And in those times I really didn't even know there'd be a future in writing for me. There was apartheid, we were fighting, you might die and that would be the end. I only did something formal and systematic for the first time when I got an opportunity while in exile. This was to study for a diploma in journalism in Berlin. At that stage I was working for 'The Voice of Women', (VOW) a journal of the ANC Women's League in Lusaka, Zambia. I went to an International College for journalism in East Germany. I truly enjoyed it, passed with distinction. I enjoyed reportage the most, it was lovely.'

'Was the instruction in English or German?'

'It was in English as it was a special course designed for practicing journalists from Third World countries. In my class I was the only person from the ANC, there was a man from SWAPO and one from the PLO and the rest were journalists from countries like Ghana and Nigeria, Costa Rica, India, Egypt. There were three 'struggle journalists'. That was the first time I did something formal around writing as a career. And when I finished studying, I returned to Lusaka and switched over to radio, to Radio Freedom. So when I came back to South Africa in 1990, because I was now a journalist [laughs in self-deprecation], I did media [propaganda] work. That's how I got to meet a lot of journalists in Joburg. But then I dropped that because my number one mission was to complete my degree – I'd been expelled in 1984 [from University of Zululand] and I had one semester to do. When I finished that, I chose to return to Joburg because I'd applied for a job to coordinate the writing of a women's health book. I thought this would be in line with my writing dreams. I got the job; it was with an NGO called Women's Health Project (WHP). It was a great fit because of my initial training as a nurse. By now, the journalism diploma had revived my desire to be a writer. I started at WHP in December 1991 although once I was there the strategy changed and we employed someone else for that position'.

'Why were you an activist?'

'Why? [somewhat shocked] 'The question is why wouldn't I have been! I think if you're Black in this country you had to be. I know some people didn't do that, but that's how I felt, there was no ways . . . I couldn't be . . . I had to do something. I think I would have had a big problem with my conscience if I hadn't . . .'

'Was there a parental influence in that?'

'No!'

'So it was your own heart that led you there.'

'It was my own heart. There was no parental influence, no sibling influence; it was just me seeing the world. I knew I had to do something. I would say that besides my lived experience, the books I was reading were pointing to one direction only. If you're conscious, you do something about it. If there's something wrong about apartheid, do something about it. If there's something wrong about the way people treat you, do something about it. Reading was also an integral part of struggle and it is the only thing I have done voluntarily, consistently, my entire life'.

I ask Khosi whether she's ever written any thing in prose.

'As we speak I'm working with an editor, Helen Moffett, finalizing *Running and Other Stories*, my collection of short fiction which will soon be published. I wrote my first novel in 2000, but it wasn't published then, so I put it aside. There is a publisher who's interested now. I also write creative non-fiction, I've had essays published in anthologies. My long term project is a biography of Noni Jabavu who wrote *Drawn in Colour* in 1960 and *The Ochre People* in 1963, both published by John Murray in London and later by St Martin's Press in New York'.

'So you're writing a biography of a woman's champion?'

'Yes, a woman, a writer pioneer. People at this stage only know me as a poet because of my published poetry books'.

'But your ambitions are wider?'

'My interests are wider than that because each genre achieves a different thing. What we can't do with poetry, we can do with a short story, and different types of prose. It was only when I did my MA that I thought I could try a short story. But, I've always been very clear about life writing because looking at an individual's life allows you to delve into a broader history, the societal context, and that's exciting to me. So if I were to really pick my genres of interest, it's poetry, short fiction and creative non-fiction – the long narrative, essays in particular, and life writing such as biography and memoir. I love those but am keen to experiment with other genres.'

I suggest that Khosi's progress as a writer can be compared to her immersion in black consciousness, one thing building upon another, development, growth. Khosi nods. I ask what life without poetry would be for her.

'Now that I've been in it? [laughs uproariously] It would have little meaning! I had a few poetry books on my book shelves but after *These Hands* came out, I suddenly thought, actually I must read a lot more poetry consciously, systematically, deliberately. And the more I read, the more I loved the potential of poetry. I love the way it speaks to the heart. I love the way it will . . . isn't it interesting? . . . actually bring you to tears! There's a lot of power in that! When a poem doesn't move me it hasn't succeeded and poems can move me even if I don't get the whole meaning. I subscribe to the view that poetry is an emotional genre. Emotion helps with clarity and clarity delivers meaning.'

I ask Khosi about her reading favourites.

She protests saying 'that depends on where you are at any given point, but if you ask what books I have next to my bed right now I have *Being Alive*, published by Bloodaxe edited by Neal Astley. I have all three volumes: *Staying Alive, Being Alive, and Being Human*. For me *Being Alive* is the best of these volumes. I have Kwame Dawes's *Gomer's Song* that I'd lent to a friend, Malika, and I was looking everywhere last week and I thought, how can I lose this book? And when I remembered I'd lent it to her, I called her up and said, 'I need my book back!' because it was that time for me, Kwame time! I'm finding that the more Caribbean poets I read, the more I love them. I'm seldom disappointed, if you know what I mean? Recently I bought a Derek Walcott selected poetry collection. I'm also rereading *The Rhythm Method, Razzamatazz, and Memory: How to Make Your Poetry Sing* by Keith Flynn. It's just the most beautiful book on the history of poetry in Europe and America. So these are the poets I have next to my bed right now.'

'And how do poems come to you?'

'Oh, they come in different ways, they all come in different ways. There are poems that come as voices in my head, some come almost complete and I have to just sit down and write. Then there are poems that come – like that poem I read [at our shared Melville Poetry Festival] about Frances Rasuge – via the news. Frances had disappeared and the news just kept reporting about her missing body. With that particular poem I didn't say, 'Oh I'm sick and tired of this news, let me write a poem.' I was in the mood for morning writing. I don't stick to that as much as I would want to, but I was in that period of my life, I would wake up at five o'clock, sit down and write, free write. And that's how that poem came. Because she'd been on the news for so long, it was as if she had been living in my subconscious mind for that extended period and then, bang! she was out on the keyboard. Some poems arrive, you know, via a simple line and I think, oh, that's a nice way of capturing something, and I write it down and then after some time I think, hmm, now what else can I say to add to this line? Some poems come through structure exercises. For instance, I love working in a group. There are times when my women friends and I say, let's come together and let's write. We're in each others' homes and we put ourselves through exercises, formal exercises, try this and that. Some published poems were born like that.

'When I wrote *Tongues of Their Mothers* I had just decided to teach myself actively to write poetry. I'd finished the MA but I wanted to focus on poetry. So I went and bought books, you know the 'teach yourself' kind of books that you get at Exclusive [Books]. So I had that one book and I'd just go through the exercises that appealed to me. Many poems that are in *Tongues of Their Mothers* came from that experience. So it's really about different processes at different times. The reality is that some poems take months – I revise and revise. There's a poem in my second book called *Summer* which I didn't include in my first book because it was four pages long and I couldn't quite make it work. Now and again after *These Hands* was published, I'd go back and work on it but it didn't really satisfy me. Then one day I suddenly realized what was wrong with it. I knew then what to do. It had been in the making for at least four years!'

'Let's talk about recognition. Do you think we [poets] get a reasonable deal?'

'I don't think so. I mean, what's a reasonable deal? There might be different ways of answering that.'

I chip in, 'What about reviews of your work in newspapers, in journals?'

'There are very few reviews of my work. When I have been mentioned it's in the context of something else; a comment about women poets, a comment on literature post 2000, a comment on Black women writers. The longest review I saw was written by a scholar from Botswana who reviewed *These Hands* and Lisa Combrinck's collection *An Infinite Longing for Love*, juxtaposing the two. Recently, Pumla Dineo Gqola wrote a very long essay in which she discusses poetry by four women poets – Gabeba Baderoon, Lebo Mashile, Myesha Jenkins and I. Those are the only two substantial pieces I have seen on my work. Often it's just one or two lines mentioned here and there with an equally short excerpt. When I've been on radio it's just to read and be interviewed, it takes a few minutes and it's over.'

'Have you received feedback from listeners?'

'No. I get a lot more feedback though from individuals via SMS or email, people telling me about what a poem meant for them.'

'So something is going on out there, but it's random, and if it comes back to you it's an accident.'

Khosi agrees. We note the paucity of academic involvement in contemporary South African poetry. She adds, 'I want to talk about another angle for recognition and this, for me, is making sure that poets have the time to write. When I look at journals from the USA in particular, and Britain, I notice many opportunities for poets to go and be at events, to sit down and write, to produce. That is what I want. I want the recognition that gives me time to create. And I'd love that to happen in South Africa because I think the biggest problem with creativity is time. You need to sit down and make it happen. And it doesn't happen like this [snaps fingers]. You need to work and rework and rework.'

Khosi talks about what's happening with women poets.

'I think the women who have come into the poetry scene in the recent past are a force to be reckoned with. The book on literature post 2000 has a chapter on women poets but it lumps all of them in there; nevertheless it was a good start. And I'm hoping that soon we will see more in-depth analyses of what that means and how it's shaping up. This is a very important issue for me because I've always been an activist, not only politically but specifically on women's issues. The way society fails to recognize women and when they do it's in very stereotypical ways. That's always been a thing close to my heart and it's taking a bit long even within poetry circles and among those who review and write about women and their contribution to poetry.'

I ask how she's presently earning her living.

'Well, right now I'm a Writing Fellow at the Wits School of Public Health, which means that I get paid every month to go and write. The proposal I submitted is on the history of nursing in South Africa. So that's how I'm earning my living until this grant comes to an end. It's a year-long grant and there's no promise for a second year but we know that the book's not going to be finished. My co-author and I will be raising funds for me to stay in for a second year.'

Shortly before we spoke, Khosi had returned from a two day conference organized by the University of Naples in southern Italy. We extend our 'conversation' with her impressions of the gathering which, for the first time for this experienced ANC conference attendee, featured a presentation of her own 'creative work'.

'It turns out,' says Khosi, 'that this is a group of people, mainly academics, who study Africa, Asia and the Mediterranean regions. Most of them were or still are communists who have supported the anti-apartheid movement in South Africa for a very long time. The university has an ongoing collaboration with the Wits History Workshop. The conference was part of the ANC centenary celebrations, called 'The African National Congress – between home and exile'. The first day of the conference was people talking about the ANC in Italy, which was fascinating because in all my time in exile, I had never heard of the Italian anti-apartheid movement. But there they were these communists, most of them very old, and they remembered O.R.Tambo, they had worked with Ruth First and told many personal stories on their involvement with individual ANC activists. South African historians gave noteworthy presentations on historical perspectives outside of the grand narrative.

'On the second day of our panel, there was myself, a poet, a doyen of South African literature, a musicologist and an artist who is a William Kentridge scholar. Thenjiwe Mtintso, our Ambassador to Italy, closed the conference. I chose poetry that fitted the conference theme, mostly poems as yet unpublished, and sent them off on the Friday. By the time I arrived on the Sunday it had been translated into Italian. By the time I was reading my poetry on the Monday it was coming up on screen and people had hard copies in Italian. This is another point about recognition. I thought, WOW, people were taking my work seriously. Some lecturers and students told me they had traveled from Rome to Naples to listen to my poetry. An editor of the upcoming issue of an on-line journal *Anglistica* asked me to submit those poems.

On the one hand, it was an interesting experience, because I learnt a lot about what the Italian communists had done in the name of the anti-apartheid movement, but at a personal level it was a very heart-warming and visible, not to mention international, kind of recognition.'

I asked Khosi for a closing thought.

'Not so long ago, my brother Mandla, who lives in Midrand and has a daughter, Amukele (Amu), in primary school, told me about Amu's poetry assignment. He suggested to her that she choose a poem from one of 'your auntie's books'. Afterwards he told me Amu was very excited about being in the 'top five' but more especially because the teacher asked if she knows the writer, and when she replied, she's my aunt, the teacher congratulated her on this family relationship! Now here's a little girl in grade four, getting recognition because her aunt is a poet. I just think that's very, very special [laughs]. One of my dreams is to see my poems read and used in schools and universities and this was an example of it starting. A little step, but it's great for Amu, it's special and important.'

□

This poem was a product of an early morning free writing exercise ten months after the idea was planted in my head. This happened far away from home. Sitting across a table at a meeting in Geneva a co-participant looked at my hands and said, "You have the most beautiful hands." I replied, "If you knew what these hands have done you might change your mind." I forgot about the interaction and returned home after the meeting, until that dawn of free-writing.

These Hands

These hands know putrid pus
from oozing wounds.

They know the musty feel
of varying forms of faecal formations.

They know the warmth of blood
gushing from gaping bodily spaces.

They know of mucous
sliding out of orifices.
These hands remember the metallic feel
of numerous guns
when the telling click was heard.
They recall the rumbling palm embrace
over grenades ready
for the release of destruction.

These hands will never forget
the prickling touch of barbed wire on border fences.

These hands can still feel the roughness
of unknown tree leaves
that served as toilet paper in bushes far away.

These hands have felt pulsating hearts
over extended abdomens
they know the depth of vaginas
 the opening mouths of wombs
they know the grasp of minute
minute-old clenched fists.

These hands have squeezed life's juice
from painful pounding breasts.

These hands have made love
 producing vibrations from receiving lovers.

These hands have pressed buttons, knobs and switches,
they have turned screws and wound clocks,
steered wheels and dug holes,
held instruments, implements and ligaments,
moulded monuments, created crafts, healed hearts.

These hands now caress the keyboard
fondle pens that massage papers
weaning fear, weaving words
wishing with every fingerprint
that this relationship will last forever.

☐

As we geared up as a nation for the anniversary of ten years of democracy I was painfully aware of the reflections that were filled with extreme negativity, particularly in the media. I then decided to write, just for me, what I valued about our democracy. I wrote a two column self-reflection on what had changed that I valued and why. In time this morphed into a five page long epic poem with the title 'Things We can Touch', which was also the original working title for the book These Hands. Four years later, after innumerable revisions, Summer was born and as you can see is greatly reduced in length! My nephew Siphesihle chose it for his English assignment when he was in still high school.

Summer

This is the summer of things we can touch.

Snaking queues that lead from farther than the eyes can see
to terminate at a ballot box, is summer.

It is a summer of Black children in buses and kombis,
on avenues, paths, roads and streets,
numerous like ants, going to school.

A summer of newly built houses along major highways
and a summer of women in high places, making meaning.

It is a summer of songs composed in blood,
tuned with guns and arranged in conversations.
It is a summer of songs I sing in swelling volumes.

This is a summer of things we can touch.

□

In 2005 I was asked by the Library Association of South Africa (LIASA) to write a
poem for the launch of the National Library week in Kliptown. I had never before
written a poem upon request. After a pani- stricken telephone consultation with a
friend, Myesha Jenkins, on the evening before the event, I wrote two poems My Book
and To My Librarian and went to bed after two in the morning. I took both poems to
the event and when I was asked to read I chose this one.

To My Librarian

Bones, gifts, under the tongue, Mamphela Ramphele,
call me woman, Mhudi, woman at point zero.

No sweetness here: seeing voices hearing visions, nervous conditions,
things fall apart, and they didn't die.

The shadow of Imana, the black insider, the famished road, the wrath of the
ancestors,
the quiet violence of dreams, the screaming of the innocent,
weep not child, love child, these things happen.

When rain clouds gather: head above water, desperate, never been at home,
Muriel at Metropolitan, juggling truths, living loving and lying awake at night,
a life's mosaic.

So long a letter? I write what I like, blame me on history.

Petals of blood, flames of fury, soul fire!

Gods of our time, the emperor, underground people.
It all begins, differently each time,
drawn in colour, on covers: titles, authors' names, publishers, isbn numbers.
My librarian knows it all.
I watch her smile, wish I could read her mind.
Her voice never high, her searches have results.
If not what I wanted, an even better suggestion –
Ume njalo my librarian. Oh, if I could sing…

Bones, gifts, under the tongue, Mamphela Ramphele,
call me woman, Mhudi, woman at point zero.

My librarian opened doors
to books I have known and books I have loved,
to worlds I never knew and worlds I wish I knew.
At each encounter these hands receive and say,
'My librarian, this way I salute you, in our lifetime.'

I am working on my next collection of poetry. Its working title is 'Journeying: poems of a transitional era'. The River Speaks of Ashes is in this collection and will be published in an on line journal, Anglistica. It is one of the poems I read at the conference in Naples.

The River Speaks of Ashes

I have known corpses
whole and intact
wounded and mutilated.

I have known ashes
of burnt corpses
bagged, unrecognizable.

I propelled them to the bank
for their relative to find and claim.

I listened when they spoke.
I memorized their names:
Champion Galela
Qaqawuli Godolozi
Sipho Hashe.

I have known corpses
and I have known ashes.
My name is Nxuba, but the arrivals
who never left, renamed me Fish.

☐

I was driving on the M1 from Johannesburg to Pretoria one day in March 2012 when I nearly caused an accident as the Radio 702 news reader reported that Francis Rasuge's remains had been found by construction workers while they were laying a foundation for a house. In 2006 two years after she had disappeared, I wrote the poem below out of sheer frustration. Francis disappeared on 27 August 2004 and her remains were found on 20th March 2012. The DNA tests confirmed the bones and skull were indeed hers and the family hopefully had closure when they held a funeral.

Her body has not been found

Her body has not been found.

I hear this on radio.
I see them mouth it on TV.
I read it in newspapers.

Her body has not been found.

It's been over a year now
I wish they change their language and at least say
Her body has still not been found
No, they should actually count the days and say
It's been 365 days and still, her body has not been found
Yes, I want to hear,
I want to hear the tally each passing day
In the same way they do when they celebrate: Episode 1000 of Generations! Episode 100 of
7de Laan!
They can count. In fact,
I demand that she be named Francis Rasuge, police constable Francis Rasuge.
I want to hear them say:
It's been 366 days and still police constable Francis Rasuge's body has not been found.
That's not too much airtime to add,
The word count is minimal.
But, wait, here's what I really I want to hear,
I want to hear them point out the responsible party.
I want to hear them say on radio:
The police have still not found police constable Francis Rasuge's body, 367 days after she disappeared.
I want to see them on TV, They must say it out loud as part of the lead stories:
The police have still not found police constable Francis Rasuge's body, 368 days after she disappeared.
I want to read in newspapers, in bold, black on white, on the front cover:

The police have still not found police constable Francis Rasuge's body, 369 days after she disappeared.
Yes, that's what I want, not this:
Her body has not been found.

□

*I wrote **Worm Music** in 2001 as a way of working through a relationship that was taking off with unusual challenges. Last year my niece Amukele chose this poem memorized it and performed it in class.*

Worm Music

I want to dance the tango
'cause my feet are so numb.
I want to dance the tango
'cause my thighs need to thaw,
my neck needs loosening,
my eyes need to see when they look,
my waist needs to know not to waste its twist.

Then, my arms will have no choice but to reach out,
my fingers will know to grasp
and together, we can dance
to the rhythm of centipedes.

Siphiwe ka Ngwenya

Siphiwe wears his hair in dreadlocks. I think this is important for his identity as a Performance Poet. He has gentle eyes in a strong and handsome face. The one time I shared a reading appearance with him, I was struck by the manner in which he held his audience in thrall. The youngsters knew him and his work well; they joined in the choruses with practiced ease. The rapport between performer and audience was spellbinding. I envied him.

Our initial interview was postponed as Siphiwe needed to attend a funeral. When we get together, I ask whether he 'performed' at the funeral? He tells me that it was a family funeral where he 'only played the drums and assisted in the singing,' but that generally speaking, 'that's how I started doing poetry. I started performing at weddings, funerals, parties, concerts, that's how I started.'

'Was that mainly in Soweto?'

'It was in many places – in Soweto, in the provinces, all over South Africa. I have also performed in countries like Botswana, Canada, the UK, Denmark, Sweden, France, Germany, Holland, Pakistan . . .'

I comment that he is widely known and appreciated.

He chuckles, modestly replies, 'I would say so, I always perform when asked. Sometimes I'm commissioned to write a poem or perform a poem dedicated to an event or a certain person.'

'Do you get rewarded?'

'It depends on the occasion. I'm paid when I'm specifically commissioned to write or perform a particular poem. But usually I wouldn't say I perform because I want to be paid. I do it for the love of poetry but I know that there are some occasions I should be paid.'

Siphiwe tells me how he was very much a self-starter in the performance business.

'I would volunteer. In the past it could be a rally or some event and I would present myself without anyone inviting me. Without even an introduction, I would step forward and perform – that was in the early eighties. You didn't have to ask permission to read your poems, you just had to be there and perform. It would not be like it was Siphiwe's poem or Mike's poem, it would be everyone's poem. In the past it was not about the poet, it was about the poem. It was society's poem, a struggle poem. If you had a poem, you could present it anywhere.'

'It was solidarity.'

'Yes, I would recite other people's poems, not always my own, depending on the occasion. I was involved in a social movement and at different times was active in various organizations like the African Writers Association, the Congress of South African Writers, (COSAW), the FUBA Academy and the Rishile Theatre Project. But now, after 1994, it's about the poet not the poem. When you attend a reading or a performance it's about Siphiwe as an 'idol', not about the content or the words.'

I ask Siphiwe to what extent living all his life in Soweto, including the most important Struggle years, has influenced his poetry.

'In most of my poems I write about stuff in Soweto, it could be an event or it could be a place like Kliptown. I write about my own life in Soweto, and how I view people and the politics but my poetry is not restricted to Soweto or Africa. It goes beyond our borders and crosses boundaries.'

I suggest that his poetry must have had a beginning sometime before he started volunteering himself to perform. 'How did it develop?'

'I was exposed to the African culture; oral poetry, praise poetry. I think that's what inspired me to get involved because I'd already heard this poetry and all I had to do was mix it with western styles. Oral poetry was part of township life. It was also encouraged at school. Perhaps they never noticed [the authorities], but at primary school there was poetry but especially praise poems for kings. You had to memorize them and then present them in front of the whole class. And also from my mother's side, the Xhosa speaking people, it could be like oral poetry or story telling. My maternal grandmother would tell us stories when we were in the Eastern Cape.'

'Which languages do you use in performances? '

'I usually write and perform in English, IsiXhosa and IsiZulu and I can also mix it with IsiSwati because IsiSwati, including Sepedi and Xitsonga, is from my father's side.'

We move to politics.

'In 1976 I was still young, I was twelve at that time, it involved me because we had poets who were political, particularly Ingoapele Madingoane who wrote *Africa my Beginning, Africa my Ending*. Especially in those years if you didn't know those poems you were out of step . . . everyone memorized them. The book was banned. But if you got the book, you could make a copy, or you could memorize it and pass it on so someone else could read it. It used to be like that. If they said, 'No, your poems are banned' then you could send it to people on tape, like Mzwakhe Mbuli's *Change is Pain*. If your book was banned you would make a photocopy and pass it on. People would pay for photocopies.'

I comment that it was like the Russian literary underground.

'There was a lot of reading, as compared to now,' says Siphiwe. 'If I were to compare to now, the reading culture is not there any more in the township. It was a compulsion that people had to read, they had to go to places. Even at home I think my parents knew, after a long time, that I used to perform. They'd hear from people, 'Hey, your son is performing, but, hau, it's dangerous. We saw him at Regina Mundi, he was performing there.' And my parents said, 'We did not know that,' because I used to sneak out of the house. Performing at Regina Mundi was great because I think that's how I grew up. I used to go there, especially on days like Youth Day, June 16 and Sharpeville Day. I'd go there and perhaps meet Don Mattera [the poet], and he'd say, 'Do you have a poem?' So he'd call me, and you'd stand at the altar, there's a crowd and you feel that now the spotlight is on you. And so you must do your job, and your job is to perform, to do good poetry and to carry the people with you. And you feel the applause, the shouting and the whistling. And while you are there on the stage, it could have been a written poem, but now, while they are applauding, you can improvise other words and they just come out. [At Regina Mundi] I'd just perform my poem then leave, I'd go somewhere else. So I'd just go to all these places.'

I mention that I once heard and watched him pull an audience into his recital.

'If it's a stage performance with an audience I like to involve them, because usually people think poetry is Shakespeare, and then they say they don't want poetry because they studied it at school and maybe it was just analyzing. So now I show them there's also this kind of poetry which you can be part of.'

Guessing that poetry doesn't yield great riches, I ask Siphiwe how he earns his living.

'I work as an administrator for the Hospitality and General Provident Fund. That's how I get something to survive.' I learn at this point, that he is married and supports two daughters and a grand-daughter.

We pass to Siphiwe's poetic ambition.

'I have one individual collection, *Soulfire Experience,* but I'd like to see myself publishing another book, or recording a DVD, because now people do listen but they want to see you when you're performing so a DVD is the kind of thing to do. People want the visual.'

Siphiwe talks about his association with Botsotso colleague, Ike Muila, also featured in this book.

'I met Ike in the late eighties, early nineties, while we were at COSAW. At that time he was at the Market Theatre Laboratory, the old one. We used to meet a lot, we used to sit and discuss poetry and recite. I'd visit him at the Market Theatre Laboratory where we'd talk about poetry and also about theatre. There would be occasions when we'd see each other perform and at the Laboratory we'd ask one another, how did we perform? And that's also how we met Allan [Kolski Horwitz] and we decided no, we wanted to form a group, a performance poetry group, a group to do different poetry styles and which uses all South African languages. So that's how we started. The first line up also had Roy Blumenthal and the late Isabella Motadinyane. Afterwards Anna Varney joined when Roy dropped out.'

I wrongly comment that as Siphiwe is so widely recognized, so well known, he no longer needs to 'push'.

'I do, I still have to! People know me but eventually they'll begin to wonder whether he's there or not there, because as a poet, you always want to be there. If you are a singer you want to be there because when you write or compose your art work you want to present it to the people. Most of the time when I write a poem, I might say it's a good poem because I've written it, but at that point I'm the only one who has read it. And when I'm alone, I recite or perform that poem and maybe still think it's good, only to find when I go out and perform it, it doesn't get the reception I expected. When I'm there, I get feedback. Some will say it's good, but others may say you can change this or that for the better.'

Ike Muila has helped Siphiwe edit his poetry. And modification comes from the interaction of Botsotso members.

'We might decide that we have a spot of thirty minutes, that maybe we have poems that are individual poems or which we would bring together into a collective poem. And we would critique one another. We'd say, 'No, it's not strong.' Or, because two poems were similar, we'd say, 'You could say it differently.' So we have the same story, but we say it differently. That's the way Botsotso works, and even in terms of using different languages, we combine them. Also we could play the drums, we could sing, depending on what we decided for that performance. We could praise God or present oral poems inspired by the black poets who influenced me in my style.'

Siphiwe tells me that in addition to being influenced by Africans, Caribbean poets and poetry are especially important to him. In regard to where South African poetry now stands, he finished our talk with these words:

'I would also say, that besides poetry being political, there's also poetry which is about love and other subjects that maybe in the past were not acceptable things to deal with. After the watershed of 1994, poets are able to express themselves more widely. Also we are free. In the past we criticized and wrote about the 'system', but now we can also check if what we've been fighting for has been achieved. If you feel that some of our aims have not been achieved you can raise this – even if you raise these things against your [former] comrades. There has also been an influence of hip-hop and rap in South Africa and I admire people who do it for good cause.'

☐

I met a woman in town (Johannesburg), bandages were wrapped around her swollen neck and legs. She begged for money, saying she had just been released from hospital. I did not give her money that moment but a few minutes later I rushed back and gave her some coins. I was surprised to see her a few days later, telling me and other people the same story. For some years now the poem has been prescribed for high schools.

BEGGING

begging has become a profession
unemployment our occupation
every soul wandering on city pavements
turning poverty into fiction
I always read words of pain
like graffiti scribbled on these sombre faces
& hidden smiles
sore lips & quivering bruised hands
who have learned the art
of lying without hurting
from those who speak diverse tongues
of the streets
of blistered hope & lynched dreams
I see them everywhere
for I am just a poet
trudging their gravel road

Kliptown is next to Dlamini 2 (where I live). I grew up doing shopping there and frequenting a movie theatre, San Souci; we called it 'bioscope' in those bygone years. It's a historic place where the ANC launched an important document, the Freedom Charter. Despite the political changes in South Africa, and more RDP houses and flats, there are still people living in worse conditions in shacks.

KLIPTOWN SHANTYTOWN

Kliptown shantytown
dreams silenced
by the morning rain
footsteps of running commuters

kliptown shantytown
the sky loses its brains
in torrents it starts to rain
people use tables as boats

kliptown shantytown
when day is young
women wash clothes down the river
children swim like fish in dirt

kliptown shantytown
frogs croak crickets chirp children snore
and nakedness entangles with passion
till dawn

☐

This is a love poem dedicated to my soul-mate. It's in English, but spiced with IsiZulu ways/style of romance. Part of its pleasure is that we can now dwell on subjects which were taboo during our struggles against apartheid. It's also a celebration of full figured or plus sized or voluptuous women.

MELI

she is voluptuous
plump queen
chocolate
    black
       dark
          brown
             sepia
magnetic brown eyes
dark luscious lips
       seductive smile
uyizihlabathi zolwandle

she is full
afrikan breasts
i cup tenderly with my hands
big ebony nipple-sharp
belly well fed
like maskandi queens

she is hips swaying
waist swinging
ample buttocks shaking
sturdy thighs shining
face glowing
legs well curved
like umdlebe tree branches
when she walks i say
unyathela ngabantwana

she is my panther
on top of umyezane tree
her mind is deeper than the sea
she can be tongue-lashing
volcanic
exploding
the last poem i compose
to propose

132

Natural Initiation is a love poem about my initiation into romance in the early 1980s. This was intimacy experienced at Schoemansdal village, in the lowveld of Mpumalanga province. It is a nostalgic poem about village life and young love. It was in those years when intimate messages were expressed through love letters and poetry. I had returned to the village after more than ten years and discovered that things had changed and most people I knew had already passed on. Bitter-sweet memories haunted me and all those values and morals had died. I also realized that it is difficult to experience true love – society is too material.

NATURAL INITIATION

while other
would-be men
trudge the bushes
of the mountain tip
to be circumsized and
advised
by their elders
who know the thorny
road of life

you woman
you woman
circumsized me
with the bitter
sweet taste of my blood
drawing images
on our lovebed
words whispered
shining
with compassion
into my ears
sinking in my heart
deeper than
the monotonous verse
of the initiator

so when i walked again
where my feet walked
many years gone by
i could feel you
and i was born again
crowing of cocks
bleating of sheep

bellowing of bulls
birds singing on trees

when the sky's tears
began to fall
thinking
alone in my room
searching deep
joyful memories
came to haunt me

☐

'Killjoy' is expressed in the voice of an oral or praise poet, imbongi or griot. It tackles social but mostly political issues like unemployment, poverty, homelessness. It questions our freedom, stirs the peoples' "frozen hearts" who thought we achieved everything in 1994. The poem sheds 'light', digging deep into reality – " legalize the truth" and be careful how you shower praise on the status quo. It is not infatuated with the"blooming lie of flowers" or rainbow nation delusions. Lastly it could fit into dub or rap or hiphop, because of its rhythm & rhyme.

KILLJOY

i am killjoy
i am killjoy

i am sad hope
life dangling on a rope
i weave warm words
cause havoc to political heads
i ignite fire in frozen hearts
i steer the mind into the light
i possess poems more sober than sermons
i move mountains
create fountains
i come like torrential rains
cleanse red stains
i am
killjoy
i kill joy
i soothe constant pain
from festering wounds
i poke

i am multitudes of drowned voices
crying out in silence
still i lose not my temper
in times of violence
stubborn words surge through me
like a piercing knife
i am poetic rich
i lose not my pitch
i spit rage on the page
i am ghetto/metropolitan/rural/oral
killjoy poet
sorrow is what i bring
red/dread/dead roots i sing
i hypnotise/demonise/legalise the truth
i see nothing fine
when the sun shines
i mock the poet singing praise in parliament
i cause a predicament
reveal poverty
in our liberty
i am killjoy
i am killjoy

i rave until i kiss my grave
i rant until i run out of wealthy words
like a river gone dry
i sigh at the blooming lie of flowers
i appreciate/retaliate/dedicate
my poetry to liberate
but i dissect my infatuation
i question liberation
i question liberation
i am killjoy
i am killjoy
i am killjoy
i am kill-joy
killjoy.

Prologue

'As the child of a Jewish Holocaust survivor, I know the pain my mother carried; a pain and depression that ebbed and flowed across her life, and as she aged, grew more acute. I carry that pain in my marrow. I also felt a deep love for her, not just empathy. For she showed that despite the odds, living could be a fulfilling experience. And because she was a woman whose natural vitality could not easily be suppressed, through her, I felt the possibilities of creativity, the transcendent power of making art.

'Evil can only be restrained if full consciousness is reached as to our choices: whether or not to do unto others as we would have them do unto ourselves – or to live trapped in manipulative, exploitative relations. I hope this sensibility is at the heart of my poetry: the simultanous awareness of the sub-conscious, the archetypal, and, if you like, the mystical, as well as the dimensions of material power.'

AKH lives across the valley in a small house in Bellevue East's Natal St. I rev up Stewart Drive. The cops are there, a favourite rousting place between Yeoville and Bertrams. AKH is tall, lean and grey-haired; we pass into his dining room to begin the interview. Born in 1952, slap bang in the middle of the 20th Century, seven years after Hitler, the Holocaust and World War 11, he's sixty years old, a long way from the turmoils of youth, but remains a passionate humanist with a particularly intense concern for social justice.

He was born in the small and very conservative Northern Cape dorp of Vryburg, but largely brought up and educated in Cape Town: Joburg is now his home. His creative talent has expanded over the years to embrace poetry, drama, song and short story writing and, hardly satisfied with this all-consuming activity, he and his Botsotso partners are deeply involved in publishing the sort of ignored, cast aside work which commercial publishers shun, significant work, important to talented aspirants without connections or outlets.

We sit and AKH pushes The Mail & Guardian aside saying he's appalled by the intelligence gulf between the magnificent Information Technology Revolution and the never-ending, blindly destructive selfishness and cruelty found in the economic and political spheres. For AKH, the two most influential and formative psychic life events were growing up in apartheid South Africa and the Jewish Holocaust. He speaks about current history as mental influence. "Whatever happens at a macro scale has massive micro consequences. The big events profoundly influence individual lives and outlooks. One wonders, what makes people capable of this sort of behaviour [genocide and slavery].'

AKH's workaday political philosophy emphasizes acts and conditions of human cooperation, unusual in the dog-eat-dog world of capitalism.

'I have a lot of respect for the term, 'comrade'. It's been bloodied and destroyed in so many ways, tainted by Stalin's Fascist Communism, but basically it's a depiction of a true relationship between people: of respect, equality and creativity. It's a matter of bringing individual talents and energy together in common purpose. That's the most beautiful situation, to experience that with people.'

We pass temporarily, from the political to the literary. With a dreadful question, I ask, 'What are the significant things in the area of the written word for you?'

Nonplussed for only an instant, AKH replies, 'It might sound like a cliché, but the core of my creativity is a fascination with stories. We are generally first exposed to stories in childhood as they capture and ignite the imagination. Language becomes a transporter of delight and beauty as well as of sorrow. A story can go anywhere – you sit there reading, or listening, and you follow the trail. Where is it going as it conjures up impressions, sensations, ideas? Yes, it was definitely the imaginative power of the story that got me going.'

We talk about the oh-so-human trait of groups gathering around the story teller since time immemorial. We talk about life becoming fictionalized in stories and moving through the world like ripples in a pool.

AKH continues, 'I've been writing poetry in the vocational sense since my early twenties when I underwent a change. This was stimulated by having to watch and deal with the mental illness of my then great love's sister. I learnt that the creative impulse carries an enormous emotional force which propels language. For me in a period of great helplessness and distress, poetry writing became an emotional catharsis which unleashed my creative power. It made me contemplate all those associations of art and madness. That's how it began and my creative endeavour has expanded and continued to this day. But after raw creation, one passes to another phase – that of ordering. I call it a sculptural process, the way one completes something, particularly in poetry but also in short fiction. By standing back, by becoming less involved, by sculpting the language to form the solid shape of the original impulse, I can watch a line achieve greater completion and independence. This process gives me enormous satisfaction.' We don't expand on this, but it strikes me that this facility is what makes AKH such a good editor.

'Who are the artists who have really stimulated you, who have got inside your head and beaten your brains,' I ask.

'As a teenager, I read mainly 19th Century European classics, English, French, Russian – Dickens, Hugo, Dostoyevsky. My mother was born in Poland. She was a complete outsider in Africa. For her, Europe remained tangible and she was strongly bound to its literature and culture. This she passed on to me but at the same time I was reading the sort of South African poetry which combined lyricism with politics. Wally Serote had a massive impact upon me and also Wopko Jensma, his work was very strong, original. I enjoyed Sydney Clouts, such polished, concentrated work which wasn't political in any obvious sense but had a powerful poetic diction. There's a long list of other poets and writers who excited me – I'll just mention a few: Borges, Camus, Neruda, John Berger, Anna Akhmatova, Doris Lessing, Ngugi, Kundera, Bashevis Singer, Bessie Head. . . this enough?' AKH ends with a laugh.

We move on to the significance of his Jewish family and politics.

'Zionism was intrinsic to my upbringing. My mother was an Auschwitz survivor but she lost her entire family. For her, Israel became a substitute for that lost family, that lost world. And naturally she influenced me. My father's family had been in SA for two generations but he, too, was a Zionist, of the right wing sort. He was also a relatively conservative if liberal white South African who didn't dream of actively opposing the [apartheid] system. We parted political company, my father and I, when I was quite young. But towards the end of his life, he saw things differently which I was very pleased about.

'He was a businessman, but a reasonable employer, he had decent, though thoroughly paternalistic relationships with his factory workers. As a kid I helped in the factory, worked with and got to know the Coloured packers and drivers – apart from our family domestic worker, the first black people I had contact with, a familiar syndrome. I have always described my dad's business ventures as being those of an "unsuccessful but unrepentant capitalist". He was almost inevitably cheated by his partners. He wasn't cut out for the hurly burly of deal-making. In general that's the way I see the commercial world – a rapacious and amoral environment. Now, of course, in the current casino capitalist environment, it's people cheating one another on a vast scale. There is no sense of ethics or proportion, so inequality has ballooned and together with that hardship.'

AKH studied at a Jewish day school, He learnt Hebrew. He celebrated a Bar Mitzvah. His expectation was to leave South Africa as his upbringing had suggested that his life would only truly begin when he reached Israel.

I ask, 'Were your parents orthodox?'

'No, they were both atheists but they maintained a basic level of traditional observance, as I, to some extent, do now that I have children. Neither of my kids' mothers are Jewish, but it's valuable for them to know something of an ancient tradition. It's an exercise in genealogy, in providing them with direct historical roots. In that regard, apart from this Middle Eastern sensibility, I'm very aware of my European ancestors and this leads me to ask, what are we, as European settlers, offering Africa? Because of Europe's undoubted exploitation of Africa, and my own privileging through apartheid, it's a question that occupies me greatly. I've written a long poem about it – a poem, I might add, which I still haven't finished! When young I didn't think of myself as being in and of Africa, but as a Zionist, albeit of a socialist tendency. That was my underlying ideology although when I was studying at UCT (University of Cape Town) in the early 1970's, I became involved in anti-apartheid student politics and my sense of being South African was deepened. But all the same, by a series of what were in some respects coincidences, in 1974 I went to settle on a kibbutz in Israel. My activist colleagues at UCT saw this as a betrayal but I was largely comfortable with this decision knowing that I had to interrogate that part of myself, to reach a conclusion, to see whether an Israeli identity was in fact my path.

'At first it was the most profound and positive experience, a great liberation. But I met Israelis who were asking what is this state of Israel and where is it going? And at the same time I met Palestinians. I worked in the orange orchards where most of the pickers were Palestinians. They came from a really poor town. It reminded me of the Cape Flats in the 1960's, the same level of poverty. I asked, what's going on here, why are people living like this? The Palestinians told me their stories and they were very open to Jewish Israelis. It seemed to me to be a time of enormous opportunity for finding common ground, for working together. But Zionism's logic is exclusive, as are almost all nationalisms. You identify the people inside your supposed camp and those outside are considered fair game, you take from them what you can. It's an impersonal and venal approach to other people, and it's not an answer, also because, as is perfectly justifiable, they fight back.'

AKH's epiphany came when as a soldier, 'round about 1976,' he was sent to Hebron on the West Bank to search the town and the surrounding countryside for 'illegal' arms. Men, women and children were herded into a square as their houses were searched for guns and explosives. He stood there facing them with his rifle and decided, 'No, I'm not prepared to do this, these people are not my enemies, there must be another way.' 'Like going into the townships,' I remark. 'Exactly!' He joined an anti-nationalist socialist group comprised mainly of new Israelis, people from outside who had a broader perception of the world.

'I must admit that we had zero influence. As for the impact of these issues on my writing, I've written about Israel/Palestine but haven't published much. However, in my latest collection *There are Two Birds at My Window* there is a poem, *Refugees*, that probes the background to the phenomenon of the suicide bomber: what is it that brings people to such a situation of desperate helplessness? I tried to understand the context and the motivation for giving up one's life to make such an extreme statement.

'And in my writing, I've also tried to look at the Jewish trauma of genocide. How does one recover from an experience like that, where your life is held to be of no consequence and you're exterminated in the most horrifying way? I don't know whether you've seen the film *Shoa* by Claude Lanzman, a French Jewish communist. Trying to understand what happened to people during that period, he forgoes documentary footage of the concentration camps to present through interviews the relationships between both the victims and the perpetrators – the extremes of human behaviour, all deeply flawed and unbalanced. The survivors were deeply damaged. No one is ennobled by suffering on that scale. And given that, when any group of people are confined to ghettos and treated as sub-human, there will be violent responses. The ghettos the Nazis pushed the Jews into, the ones apartheid South Africa constructed and the Palestinian refugee camps have obvious parallels notwithstanding the differences in the degree of murderousness. Overall, the essential deprivation, powerlessness and humiliation of being boxed in and exploited, and in many instances collaborating with the 'masters' in order to survive, applied to all three. One is not given much choice, particularly if you are providing for a family. However, for the young there is the option of resistance though this needs planning and organization and the psychological quality of being very gathered in yourself.'

I remark to AKH that his writing seems to have been as much stimulated by the politics of freedom, as by stories.

'Yes and no,' he replies. 'I don't make a distinction in my life between the personal and the political, between the work of the imagination and the task of sustaining our material selves. Those are false dichotomies. I say this because the exercise of power is vital to our lives. Power in one form or another propels us. But there's also the abuse of power that blocks us. We squander energy, time, and clarity of vision, we become clouded, we follow false gods. When I pick up the newspaper with its tales of corruption and havoc it hurts me. It angers me to think that these distortions represent so many defeated lives, where what could be positive energy is wasted in trivial activities, in irrelevance. This is where the personal and the political come together. What are we trying to achieve? That's why I seek others to work with, to work in a collective way. Capitalist individualism says collectivism is the enemy of innovation and progress. I think that's nonsense. When people are truly working together without ego, without power struggles, amazing things happen and that has changed my life and I've seen it change lives around me.

'To close off on the issue of ethnic nationalism: once I decided that I was not prepared to serve in the West Bank and Gaza I effectively left the Zionist camp and found myself traveling to Europe and committing myself to song-writing and socialist politics. Some of my committed friends saw me as a poet/dilettante but London in the late 70's was packed with revolutionary groups from all over the world – it was quite a revelation for an insular South African, there was so much to learn – and I soaked up that radical environment. But I had no desire to live in England. The overall lifestyle and climate were not to my southern and Mediterranean tastes, and in 1981 I went to New York. That was an experience of another magnitude. I formed a band, traveled a lot, met an extraordinary range of people as a taxi driver. At the same time, things were exploding in South Africa and I was very, very curious to see at first hand what was going on. I had only been back once in eleven years – in 1977 for six months – and the prospect of apartheid being challenged so widely and with such determination was too important for me to just watch from afar. I came back in January 1986 and after a few months moved to Joburg and almost immediately started working in the trade unions. I didn't pick up a guitar for twenty years, which wasn't a wise thing to do! But I found myself totally involved in what was a truly mass democratic movement. The eighties and early nineties were probably the most creative, if contested, period in South Africa's modern history and, to use a cliché but one that has real meaning, I felt privileged to be part of that.'

I ask AKH to tell me about the Botsotso Jesters and Botsotso.

'Apart from this political work, Botsotso is one of the most satisfying things that I've done. And I've only been able to do it because of working together with other people. As the Botsotso Jesters, the idea was to present contemporary poetry that covers different themes but is also socially significant without being propagandistic. We'd learn poems off by heart and present them together. We really enjoyed it. We don't do all that much performing as a group anymore but there's still the publishing aspect. Despite the problems associated with publishing poetry and short fiction, it's worth getting that sort of work out, even to a limited readership, and it's satisfying to know that people enjoy the books. As to how long we can carry on, we have no illusions about becoming financially self-sufficient. Without public funding we couldn't exist.'

I remark that without Botsotso much work would not see the light of day.

'There's a lot of important, worthwhile writing that should be recognized. I'm gratified to receive work and read it and share in it. It opens my mind to the fact that there is so much potential in human beings. People are certainly creative. All over this country there's a widespread desire to write. There's a natural thirst for self expression. It ranges from a purely private experience taking form, to receiving feedback from others. Of course, the process of art making, of becoming an artist, is a different matter. It's not simply the catharsis, the expunging, the 'coughing out' of feelings. It is the sharpening of the initial product – I'm using this term in its non-capitalist sense! – in such a way that it becomes interesting and significant to other people.

'There are many different views on how to use creativity; there's the trade of writing versus vocation. Neither is, so to speak, superior to the other. A good journalist brings something as valuable to a society as an artist. I have largely chosen to treat my writing ability as art making and I'm prolific. There are always new ideas to start developing. As a songwriter, I pick up the guitar and play a sequence of chords, and do this, over and over, till a melody starts to take shape. At bottom, you are playing with sound and you extract a melody. It's the same with words. When you write a poem, it's capricious, you have to let go. If you're writing a poem and you are more preoccupied with your desire to write the most profound poem in the world than with the poem itself, you'll more than likely produce something dull and pompous. You have to be totally focused on the poem at hand, in that almost childlike activity. That's when you feel most alive, completely immersed even as you roam the past and project into the future. You are living!

'Am I making a religion out of art? Perhaps, but it is a far less fanatical and closed world than that of the major god-driven ones and usually stimulates rather than controls. So poetry will always be a major factor in my life – reading and writing, and presenting it through performance and publishing. Losing this sense of the poetic will surely mark the death of me.'

□

A tiny woman, almost hunched over, shouting at the camera, daring the camera to take the demolition of her world – to the world. This five minute testimony remained in my mind for many days until the poem came. And it remains.

VOICE OF A HOMELESS WOMAN
Documentary of a Cape Flats eviction – destruction of shacks

At the centre

of   the

margins

a voice

in   the heart   of the storm

voice of a woman

in a frame

this

voice

of a woman

and the echo   of

hands and hammers

bringing her down

sundering

her shelter

her shack cast open

cut

d

o

w

n

hammer nailing orders

banningherspace

voice of a woman

bare

utter fucking madness

hammering down

her life

this voice

wanting ears

to cry

love

rage

you!   yes   you!

can you   help?

can you help?

One morning in early summer, after the first of the sustained rains, I was standing in my small garden. I breathed in deeply. Just a few steps away, a little bird stood stock still under a bush. Every colour filled my eyes with peace and clarity.

WATER COLOURS

Light rain after the steady beat
The storm
Clear light
Soft and fresh with dawn

Little brown and yellow bird
Still
Sheltering beneath
The green canopy of tangled hedge

White petals of a bush
Sprinkled
Across the darkened brown earth
The reddish wings

Glistening

Composed

□

This poem was, in a sense commissioned. Someone I know very well, who'd lost her way for many years, mainly because of false values, had an experience, and 'challenged' me to write a poem about it. I was at first bemused, this was the first time she had ever asked me to do this, but after reflection, really wanted to capture the essence of the situation.

BROWN (STUDY)

Brown house: bell   broom   bed

blind teacher at the door
            reaches out to the new pupil
touches her cheeks   her brow   her skull
                  moulds them into herself
then traces the inlets
            the tips of the fingers come to her
            leads them to the piano

144

                                first lesson
        feel the keys   feel their smooth glacial scope
               face the sightless eyes and wonder
               at the view within

the teacher has no need to ask
                            answers suggest questions
        and the teacher is patient
               she   guides the new pupil to each key:
                    let the note be noted
                         let the ringing tone echo

then the blind teacher hands the new pupil
a violin

               let her fingers trace the length of string
                         avoid vibration
                    absorb the tension
               that necessary stretching so pitch
                                                        e!
can rise
                    and   rise   s
                                                  i
               and   r

brown house: home for thoughtful exersize
blind bells   chime
                         sweep the floor
        the walls are uneven as they follow the curve
of the retina

the new pupil takes the blind woman's face in her hands

               she has wasted many years
out of this darkness an unheard sound will find her ear

why dwell on the past
               dischord
can become wavy
               harmonious

                         the new pupil is ready
                    she will leave the brown house
                         more than ready

The warring of creatures for survival: try to be conscious of the 'web of life', the inter-connectedness and yet distance between species. That we human beings have 'taken over' the planet imposes a serious responsibility on us – and one that we are not exersizing very intelligently. Our continuing extinction of other species is a very dubious exploitation of their habitats. Even rodents, who can endanger us, have a place. Or am I being sentimental?

INFESTATION

Don't shriek into the bushes
            sing to the rats in the garden
   calm them   make them stop prowling
                on the move   nibbling

   let those rats   almost fearless
          know the garden is not theirs to run
in this war of energy against energy
no mercy can be shown
          ultimate   almost invincible survivors
             finessing the art of engorging
they scurry everywhere   unceasing
               quick and   edgy

       what is it   they will not eat?

I watch them hustle   as I lay out poison
          bait them with shiny granules
bait them with what   they love

   slowly   I mix in grains of rice
        a little helping of gravy
                some cheese

             •

Days later
when I find a dead rat near the rubbish bin
I start
         a big furry brown and grey rat
it must be a male

        I recall this same rat
earlier   at Neville's window
    the two of us

146

watching him nibble the poison in the leaves
how he stood a little on his hind legs
      forepaws tucked up against the chest
   fellow creature with every right and need
     indeed   how could we not share
            and share a like?

this same rat   at ease
           chewing behind the glass
and now
I shudder
    shovel him into a plastic bag

☐

A glance at a semi-abandoned building; broken windows resulted in a story blown together by the elements.

THREE BROKEN WINDOWS

Across the road in the flats
three broken windows

      one a leaning tower

      one a hat

      one a tear

across the road   under a powdery vast sky
rain falls and wind blows
  and blows and blows
      into the holes

into the tower   lifting the hat   kissing away the tear

☐

Several days with a woman: the two of us traveling, surrounded by the natural splendour of the Indian ocean and the northern KwaZulu bush, and in love.

ALL

The warthog the butterfly
the waterhole the muddy brown bird
the naartjie the man spitting pips
the hemp bush
the green snake

quiet midday waves
humming
drawing
all together

The ocean the beach
the dune the headland
the scrub the lighthouse
the moonlight

hushing and drawing
together

You
woman
are the first and last curve
of light and stone and wave
as you lift your arms to the moon
and the sand on your thighs
dusts itself off

you are smoothness as flesh
and spirit is your breath
in the water
breath is your mouth
drawing me into your centre
altogether together

☐

148

This poem was originally written for an Art for Humanity project (AfH is a Durban-based NGO which tries to promote socially conscious art in different genres). The project pairs poets and visual artists, each creating a work which expresses one of the articles of the Bill of Rights. I tried to make the poem both South African and universal in application, scanning the various forms of delegitimization that victimize and diminish the humanity of those who are labeled 'outsiders' or in some way expendable, and hence become targets of abuse and discrimination.

DIGNITY

Everyone has inherent dignity and the right to have their dignity respected and protected. (Article 10 of the South African Bill of Rights)

I am the junk-and-bottle gatherer, emptying bins and so be a survivor
I am the refugee in flight, petitioning the judge not to extradite
I am the dark-skinned Untouchable who refuses to remain invisible

I am the bergie, age-old San and Khoi-khoi, now marching to the toyi-toyi
I am the remnant of genocide, the Jewish Tutsi who will not hide
I am the Cuban beard, the justice Gringo always feared

I am the legacy of Stephen Bantu Biko, the children of Soweto's hero
I am the battered wife who breaks the man-shackle on her life
I am the Living Wage rattling the boss's cage

I am the poet's conscience, rhyming against the censor's silence
I am the spat-on gay, standing proud despite the priests who prey
I am the slum-girl without a cent who won't spread her legs to pay the rent

Dignity, O dignity
You don't need a five course meal
To eat you shouldn't have to steal
Find a bed that's not of polished brass
Free the slave who wipes your arse

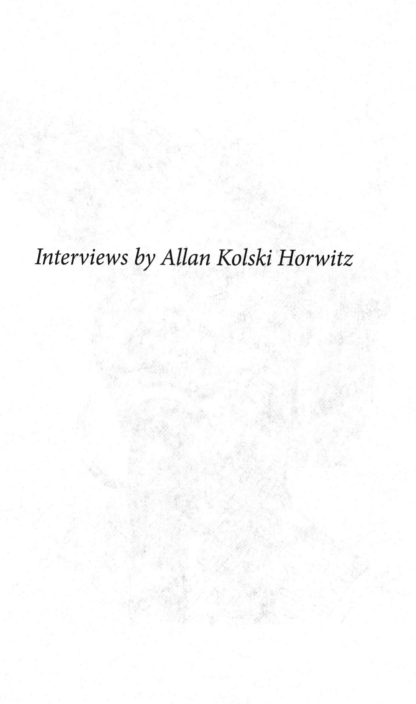

Interviews by Allan Kolski Horwitz

Mandi Poefficent Vundla

I'm sitting with Mandi in the kitchen at my house. We had first met at the end of 2012 at a poetry slam competition organized by Word N Sound productions where she'd been one of the finalists and I'd been on the panel of adjudicators – a very intriguing and stimulating task. But right now we've just come from a meeting of the Miriam Tladi Book Club that took place at Museum Africa in Newtown. There was a discussion about women and art and the small group had quite a far ranging exchange of views.

'So, Mandi, the meeting we've just come from, what did it mean to you? What do you think were the key issues and what were some of the most important responses?'

Mandi doesn't take long to get started.

'The main thing was gender equality. I remember Natalia (Molebatsi – another well known performance poet) made some interesting comments about how we, as women, are treated in poetry, like when it comes to pay, do men get paid more? But the comment from her that really stood out was about an aspect I've never even taken note of. Like, as a woman, when you are there on stage and you have guys wanting to get into your private space, shouting out, 'I want you!' I thought, this isn't an issue women only suffer with. I'm surrounded by male poets; most of my friends are male poets. Cornelius Jones when he gets on stage provokes comments like, 'Ooh he's hot'. Mandi stops for a moment. 'Then apart from this issue, there was another lady who said she's been running workshops and she can't find appropriate poems to use, and I thought 'Where have you been searching, who have you been talking to?' If I were to run workshops I know there's an endless list of poets to select from . . .'

I recall the input. 'She was a bit older than you, (Mandi is twenty-six) she's another generation. And that raises the question of whether there's communication between the generations.'

'The older generation of poets that I've experienced in my performance sphere are poets like Natalia, Myesha (Jenkins), Phillippa (Yaa de Villiers), you and Afurakan (Thabiso Mohare). But generally we're not integrated as the 'now' generation and the 'then' generation. But we are here and accessible. You can email, facebook, Twitter, all these things .Social media is our terrain, that's where you can find us.

'And there was another issue that was raised about how artists are separated – pockets here, pockets there - so how are we going to work together. And my take is that poets work with a lot of people. We do a lot of different things, we don't just do poetry. Some Word N Sound poets are helping a library in Thokoza by collecting books, also collecting clothes, helping charities. We need each other, we need to coexist. It's a matter of finding platforms where we can network and connect.'

'Tell us a bit more about Word N Sound. What does it mean to be part of the team?'

'Word N Sound is a developmental platform for poetry. It was initially a non-competitive platform but to excite people about the open mic, it became a competitive one. This is how it works. Firstly, there's a monthly session. People are required to sign up early for the open mic if they want to compete. There are fifteen slots in total, of which five are assigned to the previous TOP 5, leaving ten vacant slots for whoever wants to sign up. After signing up there's a TOP 5 that gets selected by judges, who get picked at random from the audience. The judges are given score sheets and they score their top five based on categories like performance style, audience responses, content, and so on. We don't have the same people judging every month so you can get surprises!'

'Have you ever been one of the judges?'

Mandi claps her hands and shouts out, 'No, never. I've been competing, I've always been scrutinized. But one day I want to judge, slowly but surely, one of these good old days I will judge!'

'Yeah, do that – it will make a change . . .'

She giggles and continues. 'So at the end of each show there's a new TOP 5 selected. Over the following months the TOP 5 don't have to be there early to register, there's a confirmed slot for them. But the remaining ten slots are filled on a first-come-first-registered basis. Of course, the TOP 5 could change from month to month, depending on who worked hard, which content was stronger. It's a poetry league where you score points each month until the Final, which is usually September, when we have the last open mic and then the final TOP 5 get to battle it out at the festival. There's only one annual king or queen who gets crowned. This process really does develop your craft. Some people may think it's degrading or insulting to be so competitive but it's not. I've been there and it really pushes you to work hard and take yourself to a new level. When you start slamming, you may feel like you're writing for the crowd, for people's attention. But after a while, especially when you make the TOP 5, you realize you got there because you were writing for yourself and that's why you succeeded. So it builds your character, your dedication, it builds so many strengths, and by the time you're done, you realize you have written about eight or nine strong poems in a year and now you want to publish.'

'You won the competition last year but how long has it taken you to get to that standard?'

'It was roughly two years. I remember when I started, when I was looking for a poetry platform. At that point it was still non-competitive. Anybody could just come in. It was R30 at the door. You could do what you like. I dropped out for a while but when I came back, it was competitive.'

'What made the change?'

'Afurakan, who started Word N Sound, said that the open mic was starting to get stale and he wanted to get people excited again, take things to another level. And it worked. People really prepared. The session is the first Saturday of every month. You literally start ticking off the days on the calendar. You are, like shucks, I have two weeks to memorize this new poem!'

'Every month you wrote a new poem?'

'Every month. You have to. So it really builds your character and your writing ability. When I started, I was writing 'six minute' poems, sometimes poems that were even longer. Now I write 'three minute' poems. I really critique myself when I write. *Why is that there? Is it there for you or for them* (the audience)?'

'You were writing 'six minute' poems. And then you cut down. Why?'

'There's no need for extra words. Writing's about getting to the point. Initially writing was like venting, so some lines were just unnecessary. You'd have four or five lines where you were saying the same thing. So you have to find the one line that is important in that stanza and then move on to the next. Don't rhyme for the sake of rhyming. Make your point and move on and highlight your truth. When you're done with the poem, you memorize it and that's when you find out it's a 'three minute' poem. This is just one example. Taking that whole process together, you realize the sessions are a developmental platform.'

'Did you find with the longer poems, the 'six minute' poems, it's more difficult to hold the audience's attention?'

'Yes, because some lines don't belong there. You'd have a stanza that is really tight. And then you'll have three lines that don't have to be there. We have an attentive audience, not just fools waiting for punch-lines. Thing is, people really love poetry. They are attentive and aware of what you are doing.'

'You've taken out the unnecessary, the superfluous; you've crystallized that poem. Have other finalists gone through a similar process?'

'I don't actually know, but I think they're at the same place. I listen to their poems very attentively. They're quite amazing poets, and they never write long poems. I think Masai initially had long poems but Mpho Khosi and Sbu Simelane, their poems aren't long at all.'

'Its interesting that you have this definition of what is a short and long poem and that 'three minutes' refers to the time it takes to perform the poem – not quietly read it!'

'If you do a really long poem, make sure you cover whatever it is you need to cover but never forget that you mustn't lose the point.'

'Two years ago you started entering the competitions. Had you written much before that?'

'I had. I know you'll think this crazy after what I said earlier, but a part of me feels like competitive poetry derailed me. Had I not gone through the process of competitive poetry, I would perhaps have reached this level a whole lot sooner.'

I'm taken aback. 'Why's that?'

'To be truthful, there was a point when I was just writing because I had to. Not because I wanted to. I was writing because it's like, if the next session is coming up soon, I wanted to show you that if you can do it, so can I – I'm going to kick your ass next time! So you start losing the plot, it gets blurred. Another funny thing was delivery. I also struggled with my voice. When I started poetry, without this competitive stuff, I really had my voice. But once the competition started my voice became irritating, all high pitched. This friend of mine was saying, "Can't you speak normally? When you recite, can't you use your normal voice, the tone that you're using to speak now?" It's like I would get into this other character whenever I had to recite.'

'You were acting out?'

'Something like that.'

'But it didn't work.'

'No, and then in 2012, I don't know what hit me, but it hit me, and suddenly I was just myself. Everything just came together, everything just worked and I was reciting in my normal speaking voice.'

'You were trying too hard.'

'I think so, hey, I think so. Today I roll my eyes and think, I don't know where that voice came from.'

'It's great that people are open with you.'

'Yes. Maybe it's because I'm an open person. So they can say, "You know, this is the trouble with you, this is the problem with you." And then it takes you a long time for you to actually figure it out! The good news is that once you fix the problem your poems become more real. Not that they weren't real before – people could still relate. Like, there's a poem I did called *Mother Africa*. I still need to cut out a lot of lines although it's one of the best poems I've ever written. Now I'm a different person, a better poet. I don't want to recite those old poems as they were originally written. As such I'll have to edit them, not rewrite them, then perform them properly.'

'What inspired you to write your first poem?'

'I liked to play with words. Language is cool as is the art of speaking, of communicating. The fact that I can speak to you right now in English, and English is not even my mother tongue but I can really articulate myself, there's something powerful about that. I think subliminally I've always known I had it in me but I needed to find my own approach. I loved finding words that rhyme. Ridiculous things – just put words together. I did this through school but never really thought it would go anywhere. I was in matric when I wrote my first poem, and the funniest thing is that it was the truth about my life then. As a 17, 18, 19 year old, I was a really depressed child – that was my inspiration. So poetry for me is a dark art. When I go back to my teen years, I have many files of scribbles from then. Did I ever think this would build up such a dynamic? Did I think poetry would become my life? That it would be the only thing I lived for? But it also highlights how well I've grown, so it's good to keep your old scripts. I read one and thought, "Oh, my word, I could make such a beautiful poem out of this.'

'What were the issues that were taking you down?'

'I was this chubby child. In high school I was fat. I lacked confidence. I was loud, I had no focus. I had a friend who perceived me as a spoilt kid. And she was right. I had a really grand childhood. I was a spoilt child, really I was.'

'Were you an only child?'

'No, there are three of us. My mom was a teacher at a school around the corner from where we lived, and you know how it is, everyone wants to be friends with the teacher's kids. You're Mam Vundla's daughter. There's a lot of dignity and pride there. But it's amazing how everybody could think you were the happiest child on earth and meanwhile you were undergoing your own kind of dilemmas. I've always been a chatter box. Every single report card of mine had 'chatterbox' on it. I even remember the time I had to go and see a shrink because I was talking non-stop in class, I was considered disruptive. Yet I managed to pass. I was an average kid, didn't get A's. My sister got much higher grades, but I never felt insecure. I was just the disruptive kid who had to go see the shrink – something that was also fun though. We played games, did all sorts of things. So what was a problem for the school, to me was liberation. You have to understand that we are those flamboyant kids who are lively, it's not a disease. It just means that you need to pay extra attention to us. My trips to the psychologist were once a week, in Hyde Park. My mom always reminds me how expensive that shrink was. They had to pay R500 every single Friday. And you know what R500 was in those days! Then we went on to high school which meant work. This was a serious place to be. Okay, fine, and art for me was the greatest liberator. Then at some point my parents divorced. I've always been my mother's daughter. She was more liberal, my dad was . . . my dad was really stern, too harsh for me. "This is what you must do. It's my way or the highway."

'What did your dad do?'

'He was a truck driver. When he picked us up at school in a truck, that was devastating, but when he gave us money that was cool. He spoiled us rotten back then. I remember at 1.30pm, after school, we'd have to get into this massive truck loaded with Pepsi, Stoney, all kinds of cold drinks. We used to push each other, "You must go first, you must go first!" After my parents separated I said I'm not going anywhere, I'm staying with my mom and we'll just see how things go.'

'How old were you when they divorced?'

'About 13, 14. And afterwards things got tough. My mom was learning to be a single parent. We were once spoilt by both parties, now literally there's no money. Art for me was that place where I could escape to. I never thought this poetry thing will be so dynamic. Now all of a sudden I'm in *True Love* (a woman's magazine) and people are buying the magazine and they're seeing me in it, and I'm on 702 (a talk radio station) being interviewed and carrying on.'

'This was after you won last year?'

'It was last month, two weeks back I think. I opened Tedtalk Johannesburg, and 702 was broadcasting live from the venue, this was Jenny Crwys-William's show, and after we opened the first half, she interviewed us. So it was this big thing, and then people were calling in afterwards.'

'Which poem did you do?'

'It's called 'The Rape Capital of the Womb' and it dissects the issues of hate crimes, violence against women, right now where we are and it's quite brutal. I gave the same poem to *True Love* but they only wanted 300 words so I had to chop it up.'

'*True Love*,' I exclaim. 'What a problematic name! It has to be irony, right? It's hardly 'true love' that so many women, or men for that matter, are experiencing in our society. But is this what women still want? Surely expecting an inflated romantic notion is destructive?'

'It can be destructive but the magazine covers a wide range of issues that appeal to black South African women. It's not necessarily to do with loving a man. Actually it's about carving out a free space, reclaiming your identity, loving yourself, your entirety – that's what I think the founder of the magazine was thinking, reclaiming your beauty as a black South African woman, reclaiming your black identity.

'On most of the issues affecting men and women I share the same sentiments that feminists do but my main point is not heard on many platforms. As much as I want to heal and uplift our women, fundamentally the source of the problems are men, they are the ones violating and oppressing us. If we can resolve the source of the problem, our women are going be fine. Our men are broken but what are we doing about this? This is why I haven't yet defined feminism for myself.'

'Do you deal with this in your poems?'

'Yes, I've got a poem I'm writing called 'Runaway Daddies'. But let me first say that I love Facebook, I have real friends on Facebook who open me up to a lot of issues. I was asking why so many black men are running away and I think it was Jacqueline Brown who said maybe it's because black men aren't used to being present – look at the migrant worker system. So when you go back, you see that the violation of women is actually a symptom from the apartheid regime. Black men don't know how to be present because they spent their time away from their families, and we've had several generations of absent fathers. I'm writing this poem now and I have to make a reference to her point.'

'Yes, there's certainly cause and effect, often long term effects.'

'Talking about the present without reference to the past can be dangerous. There's this random major statement that people throw around, that black people are lazy and destructive. Black people are destructive, right. I'm in a lift club which gets me to work, I travel with friends. We always listen to the radio and once, after a certain report, this is the discussion we had when passing by a location in Soweto and people had just burned down the KFC, the robots and a whole lot of other stuff. One of my friends said black people are just destructive, they don't want to work but they demand service delivery. I looked at him and said, why do you think black people are so destructive? You have to go back to the root of the problem. We were called animals. Our great-grandparents were raised as animals. We were nothing. I don't condone burning things, but I understand because there's nothing as dangerous as a hungry stomach. And what about those who make it through? The fact that you succeeded doesn't mean that the other person is not trying to succeed. Who is sweeping your streets? Who is cleaning your toilets? If you go to the locations, you must evaluate those that are going to school. When they are done with their schooling, are they looking after their families? Are they working for themselves or for their families at home? Do you send money to your mom? Are you sending your siblings to school, are you paying for your nephew's school fees? So let's go back and start analyzing the psyche of black people instead of just saying these motherfuckers are just destructive.'

'What do you make of hip-hop, American hip-hop?'

'Honestly I never grew up listening to it. Right now, there is a certain article that threw me back. There's a page that I follow called 'Truth Beckons'. They were highlighting hip hop artists who degrade the black woman. These artists are completely against dark-skinned women and keep saying how ugly they are, and the page was asking why would you support somebody that hates you? I'm not a fanatic, a hip hop head, but that got my attention. I think we, as a people, are hypnotized by the good beats and we're not always conscious of and alert to the message in that beat. So you sing along with something that is writing you off as an individual. We should listen to what these people are saying before we accept them into our spaces. We just say it sounds good and sing along – meanwhile we're hating ourselves and it's a black person telling us that we are not good enough because we're not light-skinned. I don't know what kind of racism this is but it's opened me up to very difficult emotions.'

'How do you react to current hair fashions, the weaves and so on?'

'I don't judge people by their hair.'

'But isn't this an important issue? Don't you support the black American woman revolutionary, Angela Carter, who grew an Afro as a political statement to say, 'I'm black, beautiful, proud of it, I'm going to celebrate my natural hair and the same applies to the colour of my skin in terms of not using lightening creams'. Aren't these important statements?'

'You go though different phases. I used to weave a lot. Now I'm going through a phase where I love braids, but I used to weave a lot. I'd get people who would say to me, why do you weave? You're fake.'

'Were these mainly women or men?'

'Men. Actually, it was men. They'd say, stick to your natural hair, it's beautiful. My thing is that you can't come and tell me it's not real because I have natural hair underneath my weave. You see, I have different characters. I love exploring hairstyles, hair do's. There was a point when Qhakaza (a co-founder of Word N Sound) said to me, "I've been editing your videos. In every single video you have a different hairstyle. There are videos where I don't even recognize you!" I love playing, exploring myself. I could have any kind of fibre, anything attached to my hair but fundamentally when I have my Afro out – that is me. The important thing is that after you've explored and done the rounds, face yourself. Come home to yourself. Of course, there are women with relaxed hair who will tell you off. I say to them, you apply crème relaxer to your hair and you're going to tell me about my weave! So even though I don't judge people harshly I understand the whole politics behind hair.'

At this point I make my enduring comment about saving poetry from rhetoric and cliché.

'The thing about making a political statement in a poem is that you've got to find an original angle, fresh images and ways of putting across the message.'

Mandi's response is well considered.

"If people think you're a cool poet, they start listening to your messages and taking them personally. They start analyzing themselves according to what you've said. The previous revolution was bloody but our revolution is going to be creative. If poems are beautiful, amazing, people will learn love through your poems. Right now we have this whole collective of poets. On Women's Day we filled the Soweto Theatre. The show was free and when I got on stage, the first thing I said was, oh my God, it's a full house. We couldn't get over it! I don't know where all these people came from but slowly but surely we're reaching out and the message is getting across. We, black people, are not comfortable in our own skins. That's the problem. We have to teach people, remind them of the beauty of just waking up in the morning and being yourself.'

'The main themes that you've touched on, have you chosen them quite consciously or have you found yourself writing about them in a spontaneous, almost unintentional way?'

"I don't think anything's a coincidence. Everything has always been a build-up in my head, things that I've struggled with, things that surround me. I had a poem about a break up. I took a total spin. When people heard it, they went buck wild and they still go buck wild for it. It was about a relationship I had six years ago and the effect of the break up. And it was reflecting also to my current status now as a poet and to how, when people are attracted to you, it's quite dangerous in the spoken word environment where they aren't necessarily attracted to you as a human being but to your poems – they're loving your poems and they love you on stage, so they love the hype, that everybody knows you in the poetry circles.'

'Many young poets, no doubt influenced by hip-hop, stick to rhyming verse. Do you think it has any advantages?'

"I love rhyming verse. The rhyming amplifies the content in the message and that's how it works out. But if a poem hits me, it hits me. It doesn't matter whether it rhymes or not. It's all about imagery, if you're able to take a simple emotion and make it dynamic, that means you have taken me there, and if you recite poetry and a movie is unfolding in my head, you are getting me there.'

'I love my writing, I really do. When you start with a simple word and you define it, and make it mean something else, like you would take a simple chair and the way in which you've just defined this chair turns it into something else so that I don't see it simply as a chair any more. But there are a lot of good poets. In some ways my likes are seasonal. I experience the same people at most of the sessions and they come out with something different all the time.'

'Do you think you'll start to write prose?'

'I don't know. I started trying to write reviews to see if I could break out of poetry. But the rhyming scheme is dangerous, it's contagious, it's something I carry unintentionally. Something unfolds and you're like, 'I didn't want this to be like that, this is supposed to be 'simple' writing.' But what happens when the metaphors aren't there? Can adjectives still be profound? Can you still see the images when you don't have the rhyme schemes? So I'm trying that now. I'm really trying.'

□

My translation of the inhuman violation of our women in the ghettos.

Rape capital of the womb

There's a province in the rape capital of the South African womb
where cross roads are angry at men
who declare she had cigarette loose legs.
They skuif the 15 year stompie to death,
autumn leaves her ashy feet on a winter street that
breaths heavy like T.B.
When the wind blows her body across the road like smoke,
the tar coughs up phlegm to clear her skeleton from its chest.
Then summer sweats her death like granules of malaria on the pavement.
The seasons are contracting fever by day,
a chronic disease called rape floating in the air
and it's worse than Aids.
The cd4 doesn't count yet
just the number of men you've slept with.
Questions will feel like knives held against your cunt
probing, are you sexually active?
Yes!!! Will sound the alarm.
The sirens will raise their frowns
but the ambulance won't come.
In the private parts of our ghetto
there are cervical wars.
Under wears are under attack.
A city of cavity walls crumble
from the drones in your balls.
Street lights watch
vaginas tear at the fence.
There's a cycle of menstrual men,
bleeding women at their gates,
where yards tell double stories
of rape on one acre of land.
Her body lies bent like a crescent,
no u-turn for the uterus
so the gutters drain Noxolo Nogwaza's pelvis.
Listen to her name, it's a peace sign
getting stabbed at the end of its phrase.
Her soul has reached a dead end
in a town called Booysens,
Anene, a dilapidated building sky scraping statistics.
Can you imagine the view from the windows of her soul
when Bredasdorp let her perpetrator walk

over his sins like a bridge built on the breaking backs of women
who stood like pillars against chauvinistic odds?
You strike a woman, you strike igneous rock.
We will burn these tombstones
where we're slaughtered like sacrificial goats
served to patriarchal Gods
who hold our bodies like oaths
at the temples of their groins.
We're sworn to serve their testosterone.
When graves set the tables and hate crimes are seated,
where bloody napkins wipe their feet on table mats
laying a cutlery of bones besides shovel-like spoons,
where bowls fill like tombs craving bodies like you,
will your skeletons get out the fucken closet?
Where gay pride is hung by gender violence
there are exorcists casting demons with their penis
from the bodies of lesbians,
queens dethroned from the earth.
There are ghosts of girls clinging to umbilical cords in court
waiting for justice to be served.
Dear lord, deliver us like babies away from this morgue
where mothers carry body bags in their stomachs.
The child kicking in the rape capital of the South African womb
could be you.

☐

This is how our family fell apart. I'm grown enough to accept the shattered pieces.

FAMILY MATTERS

I'm tired.
My arms are stretched out loud
because my body is yawning.
My tongue, stoned with rocks
from digging the truth,
promised the grave to never let my dreams rest in peace.
It kills to speak the language of the dead
so I lay dead awake.
It hurts to think, the body of my mind aches,
my corpse is straight,
my neck bows at the temples of my head.
I should be sleeping
but I toss and turn towards demons,

eyes open doors to question evil,
my bed, a coffin
where every night a piece of me dies quite often
from the day
sinking mother into debt.
The deepest story of my grave
has me reading between my lifelines.
Just to catch my breath,
my diaphragm has turned frisbee in my hands.
Coz breathing is a game of fetch
our lungs never know if air will come back to our chest.
My mattress, a pavement
waiting at the stop sign for the nightmares to end
in prayer –
our father … had left our mother.
So I bowed my neck at the temples of my head
but my knees aren't there.
They dangle while my soul's on an armed chair,
hands fold in mid air,
my body's still not there.
I surrendered my carcass to blood,
it's thicker than water.
Still water runs deeper
than the bond our house failed to hold.
We drowned behind these walls.
Our roof leaked from holes inside our hearts
doors couldn't shut up.
Handles carried us from hand to mouth,
the lever arched
when they bent the truth to keep our family straight
but the marriage had a jagged edge
till death do us part they said.
I died when they parted ways,
made it to heaven on my rollerblades but
that cut my heart in 2 paths.
The one road turning me 12 years old from hell,
no candles to blow the pain from the cake
so I couldn't make a wish
when my parents did the splits
and I ripped down to my siblings.
We were just kids
playing Tshigago on the streets,
picking a team
wasn't choosing mommy over daddy.
It was finding the strongest link,

someone to duck a ball whilst stacking a pile of tins,
the trick, make it home without getting hit.
Then it hit me:
I had no home.
A strange board wrote "this house has been sold."
Mother did as
she did as she was told,
packed her skeletons in our wardrobe.
I wonder when my baby sister plays house
does she believe in landlords or a Jehovah's Witness spouse?
Does Jehovah witness the scars
blacklisting her arms
from scrapping the cents to pay her piggybank and the rent?
Is she living off borrowed bread?
Does she scramble the eggs from her menstrual cycle
just to put food on the table for a period of staples,
to clip pieces of herself torn apart by loansharks?
A friend said white families leave their kids investments,
when ours hit the grave
they bury us in debt.
So black child before you be wed,
we need a 3 months bank statement,
proof of engagement and proof of payment.
I'm sorry, we regret to inform you
you can't get married in community of property because the bank owns your wife.
Mr Vilakazi please
settle your account.

☐

*A friend's most treasured secret spilled amongst three women. We listened; I absorbed
then wrote.*

BASTARD SONS

Her ovaries keep hatching a bastard son
raising beautiful flowers
a bundle of joy
that wilts before birth.
When pregnancy is that secret you don't want to keep,
so you kill its rumors
and here say speak in cavity walls with ears
drumming kicks and screams to the floor.

Tom's vocals slurred in the umbilical cord that strings his dead beat.
What will his ghost speak when he and his protruding siblings meet?
Will they shake the spirit of Tom's chopped hands?
Tying fallopian tubes into ribbons inside her womb
to remember that he was once a gift from God's agenda
grown in the wrong placenta.
Coz Santa's Clause had floors
Tom was delivered though the wrong door
he couldn't fit into their world
so they broke his limbs to bits
this puzzled pieces of Toms kindred spirits to unrest
and now he wonders, like Alice
in no man's land
chasing demons inside semen to man up to their erections.
It takes a second to come
but a lifetime to raise a son.
Tom, short hand for Tomb,
this is where she plants her ovum.
A hysterectomy was overdue
so they excavated her womb
digging fetal bones that were never traced to patriarchal homes
coz they hadn't begun teething.

Ashes to ashes,
uterus to dust,
every single day a fatherless skull gets crushed
and all that remains
when the sonar scans the grave
is a casket of lust
lowering a mother's love deep inside the ground
where her ghost child
begs the street to show him the path of his father's prints
so he can say
before he finally rests in peace,
I've got my daddy's feet.

□

To date is actually seven years ago, reflecting back on my most treasured relationship, wrecked by a message read out of context in comparison to my recent standing with men. I'm finally brave enough to own that tragedy.

6 YEARS LATER

I'm finally brave enough to write about you!!
I've kept your story in the draws of my stomach
there are shelves
where folded memories are broken neatly in half.
I've searched for you pieces in the past.
My relationships have been puzzles I'm too broken to complete
so I let them go.

The way you let me go
like a scream swung aggressively in our conversations
when you threw accusations like stones
I was caught in the rubble of you words.
Some mouths open like graveyards
ready to talk you in.

There are 6 years of syllables
that still pronounce your departure
leaving my tongue like careless speech
running your mouth like baths of water
down my desert's spine.
I am empty tubs drained by love
I can no longer drink from you hugs,
at each other's throats
like lumps with oxymorons.

Agreeing on our differences
though we were alike
your love was amazing
your jealousy was clumsy
but you loved me.
I can't settle for those attracted to my poetry!
I am more than just a good dam poem
when I leave this Poetry stage
there is still the rest of uMandisa left.

No figure of speech can help you figure me out
coz there is nothing Poefficient about choosing my lines over my heart.
You leave it empty.

I am granules of drought
a vacant body of space
where some men think they can visit only to vacate.
My body is no holiday sin.
The room in my heart is fully booked out.
I've learned the hard way
to hold my breath like clutch bag
with broken accessories of self.
Purse my lips together
whenever I remember
your kisses, the flavour of peaches
before the worms began to sprout,
spoiling the fruits of our love.
You're still the rotting apple of my eye.
Your heart as cold blooded as reptile.

When his soul rattles your body like snakes
there will be no cage to bar you from the monster you will become
you will hear the wolves howl.
Do you hear the wolves?
They're calling for beasts to unleash the monsters inside me,
coz I've loved you wildly
like animals that eat their young
I swallowed my pride of lions,
roaring like dinosaur thumps in my Jurassic heart like shepherd.
I'm herding my emotions away from your sting
I'm a swamp of feet ready to shed my calloused skin and flee
to the beginning of my 6 year hive
to suckle the honey I was cheated of.
When relationships leave before takeoff,
the heart of your ocean becomes a lonely sea
where a school of fish won't teach you to swim.

Waves will no longer greet
shells will no longer speak
the echo of whales bigger than your cries.
Love bites worse than the sharks,
if you're fishing for my heart
prepare for Noah's arch,
I am floods of angry love
so bring his animals to tame this jungle of a farm
I have recently become
a barren human field
no longer growing in love.

MIKE ALFRED

I am at Mike's house; an expansive, high-ceilinged dwelling on Langermann Kop that affords a wide view of Bez Valley. Ever hospitable, he and Cecily (his wife of fifty odd years) have more than satisfied me with chicken curry and salad and several glasses of full-bodied red wine. During the meal we had a wide-ranging and spirited discussion, but now the two of us settle down to a more formal interview while Cecily adjourns to watch tv in the living room. Interestingly, our beginning point flows from an earlier topic concerning courage and integrity. In this connection Mike had mentioned that he wanted to tell me about the only time he had heard Jacob Zuma talk live; this had been in a Luthuli House conference room.

'The context was that Zuma had said something that praised Afrikaners and ran down the English speaking South Africans. I had gone in there not expecting much, but Zuma was charming – as Zuma can be – and the conversation was entirely one sided. He was talking about the land belonging to 'everybody' or some bloody nonsense like that. Having come away from it I was appalled by my cowardice. I was appalled that I didn't ask him why he was praising the Afrikaners and giving the English speaking South Africans a bad time. This was just before he became president. In fact, he was leaving that meeting to be let off the hook for all his skullduggery. His sentence was being waived; he no longer had to answer to the law. But it wasn't him that I was really getting upset with – it was me. I didn't challenge him. You know, as a person, as a citizen of this country, as a citizen of the country I belong in.'

I nod then interject, 'How do you think poets should deal with this political reality or any other for that matter?' and Mike answers, 'I think they should be as honest as they can be in their writing of poetry. I don't think they should suck up to anybody or any ideology.' I nod even more emphatically and follow up, 'So how did you stand in that whole debate in the 80s, the one about 'standards'? If you recall, people like Steven Watson were very forthright, saying that all the new political poetry, mainly by young black poets, was very poorly written, was just rhetoric, didn't qualify as poetry per se. What was your take on that line?'

'I agreed. I agreed, and I agreed not through my own voice, but when I wrote my book *Johannesburg Portraits* in which I interviewed Lionel Abrahams who was a mentor to me. Incidentally, he expressed the same opinions and I was very happy, I was very happy to put those thoughts down in writing. I was never terribly impressed by a lot of the black protest poetry. I thought it was badly written. It was repetitive. Everybody was saying the same thing and getting on the protests and the freedom and the amandla and anti-apartheid bandwagon.'

I take another mouthful of wine. 'Do you not think it was inevitable that a new generation of young black people would seek some literary expression for their challenge to the system?"

169

'Absolutely, I can't argue with that.'

'And if that's the case, did 'white poetry' deal with that sympathetically?'

'You're giving me a hard time, Allan. I don't know how 'white' poetry should have dealt with that. I was busy living my own life. I was earning my living. I was doing what I could with my *Manpower Brief,* we're talking about 80s style, in trying to present a view to whites, that blacks should be heard and blacks should be incorporated into the economic world and be given opportunities. So I wasn't operating to any great degree in the poetic world. I was operating in the professional world of industrial relations and human resources. That's when I started my *Manpower Brief.* I was writing poetry but I don't remember, I'm sorry to say it, I don't remember what I was writing in the 80s. I'll have to go back and have a look at what I was doing. But I was publishing. I was publishing all over the place . . . *New Contrast, New Coin,* Lionel Abrahams' *Sesame.'*

I resume my 'historical' questioning, 'What was the tone of those magazines at that time? What sort of work was largely being published?'

Mike replies, 'If you look at *New Coin,* under Robert Berold at that stage, it was the early 90s, the tone was very 'freedom', was very political in terms of the state of South Africa. And I wasn't writing political poetry though I wrote a poem about Slovo which Berold loved, that was very political. But it wasn't . . . (I am tempted to jump in, remembering the poem – it was a very lyrical, humanist piece about Slovo walking his dog, Slovo as an ordinary person, neither the 'hero of the masses' nor the devil of anti-communist whites, but Mike continues) . . . 'It was about Slovo's short freedom before he died of cancer; about what he had to do by coming back to South Africa. It must have been an exceptional poem in Robert Berold's eyes. It was the only one he published in his anthology *In the Beginning.'*

'He didn't publish your other work?'

'Yes, he did. But I was quite surprised. I'm just not that intellectual. I write poetry that comes into my head. I get an idea and I write it. And a lot of that comes out of my experience, my reading, being a white South African, and it might turn out, might appear in some ways to be political when really it's almost an accident.' Mike pauses, then adds, 'Although I must say my poem *Ah Jo'burg,* about a black person coming into Jo'burg, and having a hell of a time to adapt and settle down and earn a living, to survive in fact, was very consciously political but it could also be seen as sociological.' Another pause. 'You know, some of my stuff has a sting in the tail and even I'm not quite aware of that when I'm writing. But I suppose I know I have a bent for irony.' Mike leans forward. 'Can you turn that off for a moment?' (He's referring to the tape recorder on the table.)

I joke, 'You can keep talking – it will be edited.'

Mike laughs, 'Okay, so you can take this as an aside to my writing. I wasn't too happy about this interview. I thought it probably didn't have a place in our book. There would be too much of Alfred's ego in the thing. But Cecily was happy, she said, yes, go ahead.'

It's now my turn to laugh. 'Aha, the boot is on the other foot! We mustn't pretend you're some kind of omniscient interviewer exempt from being grilled!' Then I pick up the interrupted thread. 'I know I'm belabouring the point, but to go back to this issue of our history, the fact that, through Staffrider in the mid to late 80s, there was a veritable explosion of young black writers . . .'

'That was a terrible magazine, I hated it.'

'That's what I wanted to ask you, your thoughts.'

'Staffrider was the producer par excellence of that sort of protest poetry. I couldn't stand it, and I . . . I had an emotional response to bad writing. Not necessarily the politics, but just bad writing, repetitive stuff that came through again and again. I've already said this.'

I refuse to give up, 'But you know, if one looks at our history, I'd say it was inevitable. There was no way that a young generation who had taken quite a conscious decision – liberation before education, liberation before anything else – could have done anything else. They were saying, 'We've just got to get this monster off our backs, prioritize this struggle so that we can one day really live and develop as human beings.' I pause before adding, 'We poets, as much as anyone else, should understand this: an historical current needs to find its expression, and the form may be quite awkward and repetitive but it's objectively necessary. Would you not say that's a fair comment?'

'Absolutely. I can't argue with that as an evolutionary aspect of, or the offspring of protest. Physical process, the intellectual offspring, and we were all caught up in the times, and I was hopefully doing my bit in other areas, and also to be totally honest, in fact, you know, I'm this conservative whitey who likes literature, and looks at poems with a critical eye. Doesn't matter what sort of poems they are. I look at them analytically. What a thing to say. But I do. That's me.'

I home in for the kill, 'You would have seen yourself in the 80s as being conservative in most respects or just politically, that is conservative in your lifestyle as well?'

'Ja.'

'Thirty years down the line, how do you view that?'

'I'm still quite conservative. You know, my political opposition took strange forms. I was a professional human resources manager and consultant and my action took the form of integrating facilities at the Modderfontein factory. I was known for quite a famous phrase, 'All shit smells the same'. I was trying to get decent facilities for the black workers at the plants. The white guys had black helpers. They were snuck in on the budget just to look after the white toilets and canteens and eating rooms on the plants. The black facilities were shocking. But nobody gave a fuck. I changed that. I helped to change the accommodation and other things. I became extremely unpopular with my managerial colleagues. And then, later on, I started the *Manpower Brief* and it was very, very strong in terms of the message that corporates needed to start developing black staff. One of my most significant discoveries, as a result of this journalism, was that black foremen played an enormous role in industry. They were interpreters. They were interpreters of the white boss and they were interpreters of the black workers, right in the middle, and they were doing the most amazing, unrecognized job. And I was interviewing people like black professionals who were struggling in white organizational culture and that sort of thing. This was my contribution, there in the work world. I suppose what made me different from many white managers was partly my own personality, but also there was a positive culture among human resource managers. A lot of guys were involved, quite deeply. I mean one of my great friends was the personnel director in the 80s of Eskom. He was a dyed-in-the-wool Nat but he changed. He became involved with the trade union movement, started challenging his bosses and started the German system of union representatives on the executive. And there were a lot of people, a lot of HR managers who were busy doing, once again I would say, unrecognized, but important things.'

'But it didn't directly infuse your poetry.'

'No.'

In the face of this flat statement, we both pause. Yes, this theme has definitely been exhausted! I open up a new area, something more domestic.

'You were born in 1937. Where?'

'In London.'

Chuckle. 'Ah a soutie!'

'No, I'm not a soutpiel but my father was. He moved back and forth. I came here as a toddler and apart from living in London after Cecily and I got married, I have been here all my life.'

'You've never regarded England as your home?'

'Now that's also a difficult question. The answer is yes and no. As you know, I've written books about Johannesburg. In a crazy way I grew up with a sense of place but the place wasn't Johannesburg. As a result of my mother's terrible homesickness for London, I thought Johannesburg was a suburb of London and when Cecily and I went to live there, I found my way around as if by magic. It was magic, but by and large, it transposed itself and I became very involved in Johannesburg and its fascinating history and space and everything.'

'What made your parents emigrate?'

'The Great Depression. My father lost his job and he was offered a job here. But he wasn't a stranger to South Africa. In fact, he was born here. My grandfather came to SA just after the Anglo-Boer war and spent many years in business. He joined the IW Schlesinger organization, got married here, had all his children here. They lived in Camps Bay, my father went to Sea Point Boys High. But then his father sent him over to England to the London School of Economics where he failed miserably, silly bugger. Afterwards he worked in London for a long time, married my mother and had me. Then in 1937 he lost his job and couldn't find another. He was an advertising salesman and they came here, but their sort of newfound economic freedom was short-lived. The war started and he joined up. He spent from 1939 to 1943 in the forces, not very far away, at Germiston Rand Airport. He was in the air force, in charge of technical stores.'

I butt in, 'Did your parents guide you politically? I mean, what underlay your taking the 'high road' in the 80s and pushing for a colour-blind equality?'

'Dad was liberal, broadly speaking but he was a contradiction. He was a Rand Daily Mail reader, a big thinker, though his behaviour towards black waiters at a restaurant was too terrible!'

'So in your home you were exposed to essentially liberal values that came to constitute your moral foundation?"

Mike guffaws, "No, no. My mother wasn't liberal. She spent her life moaning about the blacks.'

I can't resist a dig. 'That was an occupational obsession of white housewives!'

Mike backtracks, 'My father was quite well educated though he really screwed it up. He was a well-educated, intelligent man. My mother was very intelligent too, believe me. They taught me to read at an early age and they both had wonderful vocabularies. I was very aware of words.'

At last, a clue as to where the poet came from. 'There were lots of books around?'

'A lot of books around, yes.'

'And your siblings?'

'No siblings. I was an only child.'

I stop. This could be interesting . . . 'Is it peculiar or awkward to be an only child?'

Cecily interjects from the other room, 'I'm an only child as well.'

The plot thickens. 'Both of you! So the "only children" got together! What's your view on that? Looks like you decided to correct the imbalance – you've got three children, right?'

'Two and four grandchildren.'

'What do you see as the merits or disadvantages of being an only child?'

'Too much loneliness, too much introspection. Too much of a literary life possibly. Too much reading.'

'Did you feel isolated from your schoolmates?'

'Partly.'

'Do you think of yourself as a loner at that point in your life?'

'I think I've always been a loner to some degree.'

I shake my head. 'You don't give that impression.'

'I mix very well. I can be friendly with anybody. But I do have a secret internal life.'

'That goes for all of us. But it's not as if you avoid human company?'

'Oh no, I enjoy it greatly.'

'But in terms of bonding with people, do you think being an only child affected your ability?'

'Well, not negatively. In fact, it might have affected it positively, because I was ready to be outgoing. But, you know I had good friends throughout school though I've always seen myself as a bit of an outsider.'

'Let's unpack that a bit more. There's the romantic myth of the artist as the outsider – he or she who doesn't fit in with conventional life, the artist as bohemian, as visionary or mystic. How do you see yourself in terms of that kind of paradigm?'

'Let's deal with that practically. There was no religion in our home. But when I went to prep school I suddenly attended RI (religious instruction) classes. I went home and asked my father some questions about God. And he said, 'Listen, if you meet God in the street, or anywhere else for that matter, please bring him home to dinner. Because there are a few things I'd like to discuss with God'. So I was brought up as an atheist. Quite, powerfully, too – militant atheist. I was a bit gung-ho during my school years and later I influenced somebody in the army and was quite ashamed because he was such a nice guy and such a good Christian. Yes, I was a bit ashamed of myself...'

I am astonished. 'Why ashamed?'

'For making him... doubt. I challenged his beliefs. Why couldn't I just have left him with what he was comfortable believing?'

As a confirmed "unbeliever" I am taken aback. 'Do you think that if people hold onto illusions this justifies their happiness? In other words, that "ignorance is bliss"?'

'I don't know whether it's illusion. Some people get quite a comfort out of religion.'

'Some people get a comfort out of having a bottle of whiskey a day!'

'That's true, but I quickly reached a different stage after that. I didn't interfere with people's beliefs. I had my own. They were quite powerful and they remain powerful to this day. My dad was a bit of an iconoclast as well. He'd challenge ideas and thoughts and I followed that particular part. From that point of view, I'm not a man to be in the popular mainstream, but not an opstoker either. Quite passive, not an activist.'

'You've never been part of a movement, an organization, a party?'

'God forbid! I'm not a joiner.'

Cecily chips in, 'He wouldn't join any marches. For absolute sure.'

'I joined one march at Wits. One of the academic freedom marches.'

'When was that?"

'In the late 1950s. It was led by Philip Tobias. It was one of the famous ones. And there I was. Amazing.'

We both drink more wine. I pause a few moments, decide to go back to the subject of poetry.

'When did you start writing consciously as a poet?'

'For a long time I didn't think I was a poet.'

Cecily can't resist another intervention, 'You always wanted to be a journalist.'

Mike doesn't bat an eyelid. 'Yes, I always wanted to be a writer. But it only started to happen much later in life. I was in my late 30s and I started journalism in my early 40s. So it was late in life. Human resources was my occupation – and a very stimulating one.'

'That is unusual. What pushed you to come to poetry so late?'

'I just had to do it. It was a compunction.'

'Did anyone influence you?'

'No.'

'It just suddenly came upon you?'

'I just had to do it, it erupted.'

'Was there any particular emotional upheaval at the time that pushed this?'

'Yes, there was. You know I quite enjoyed poetry at school but they made you memorize it. I was always the first one to have to get up and recite because the teachers never remembered who was the last to have recited, and went straight to me at the top of the alphabet. So that was all my exposure – and I quite enjoyed it, and, in fact, I did a degree in English, three years of a BA. But to come back to an early stimulus, one day I read quite by accident, *The Death of the Ball Turret Gunner,* a five-line poem by Randall Jarrell published in 1945. It's about the death of a gunner in a Sperry ball turret on a World War II American bomber aircraft.'

Mike gets up from the table. I have a sudden intuition that I'm in for a treat – he is going to fetch the poem! And, indeed, after a few minutes he returns with a well-thumbed book and reads:

> *From my mother's sleep I fell into the State,*
> *And I hunched in its belly till my wet fur froze.*
> *Six miles from earth, loosed from its dream of life,*
> *I woke to black flak and the nightmare fighters.*
> *When I died they washed me out of the turret with a hose.*

He sighs. 'It blew my mind. Absolutely blew my mind! Is this what you can do, with words, with poetry, with modern poetry? But it remained dormant for years and years. And then, anyway, I was never consciously a this-or-a-that poet. It was a non-intellectual activity. Really I didn't give it much thought, I had an idea in my mind, and I wrote about it. And eventually I went to Lionel Abrahams and he had a look at my stuff and published a bit of it and told me to use more punctuation. And I sort of . . . I sort of went on from there.'

'Did you take his advice?'

'Yes I did.'

'And adopted a more formal approach? Was this in the 80s?'

'It was the late 70s.'

'Do you recall any others who were in that class, or group?'

'I didn't attend his class then, I just wrote and I went to him one day and said, 'I'm writing poetry, here's a little anthology, I'd be very grateful for some feedback and guidance'. I must say I was very frightened of how I would deal with his disability, and I had difficulty hearing him because of his faltered speech. But you know, like I guess pretty well everybody else, I grew very fond of him, and his selflessness, his desire to help. I attended several of his famous Monday night groups much later.'

'Did he in fact influence the way that you are writing, beyond of course the question of punctuation?'

'Not to any great degree, I don't think. In the early years of my writing poetry, I don't think anybody really influenced me – which is not good and might well have been bad. But later on, when I started reading from all over, poetry in translation, the American moderns and post moderns in particular influenced me.'

'Any particular poets that stand out?'

'There was Robert Frost whom I just loved and the San Francisco drunkard, you know his name, the guy who couldn't get published . . . Charles Bukowski. Also Ferlingetti I liked very much and Anne Sexton and the New York poets, Donald Hall among them. I just love them and read them again and again. I've got a book on my bedside table.'

'For your BA you were studying English literature?'

'The romantic poets, we did TS Eliot which I find too intellectual but fascinating.'

'You never consciously modeled yourself on anyone else's writing?'

'No.'

'What about South African poetry at the time?'

"Douglas Livingstone. Some of his poetry was really great. And Clouts, I read and enjoyed. And obviously "Where's the bloody horse?" Roy Campbell. I read him and that sort of thing.'

'Did you enjoy Roy Campbell?'

'Yes, partly. In general I found him heavy, sometimes difficult to follow, too long. But I wasn't conscious that anyone was influencing me. In some ways I don't quite know what this means.'

'Did you read work in Afrikaans?'

'I have read a little but never in an important sense.'

'And now, today, you read much contemporary poetry?'

'I really concentrate on the work that comes through in Botsotso as well as the work that's in Gus Ferguson's Carapace. Gus publishes me often. I really value him.'

'What's your general sense of the poetry in Carapace or Botsotso?'

'Botsotso includes a lot of black voices, and there's still a lot of protest poetry but it's a far more sophisticated presentation of poetry than the old Staffrider stuff. There's a far wider array of poetry and it's not all political. It's about love and life and violence and you know, there are some very interesting voices there. There are some very interesting white voices as well like Rosamund Handler. And *Carapace* has pushed some very fine poets, Finuala Dowling for instance I think debuted there. And to his great credit, Gus also publishes some of the old classics like Douglas Reid Skinner and Patrick Cullinan, who died recently.'

I agree. 'Patrick Cullinan was a very fine poet.'

'As I've become older, I've become more immersed in poetry and during my retirement even more so in the reading and thinking about it. Poetry in those early days was really a hobby, an adjunct to my life, to my earning a living. I didn't think about it analytically.'

'And now you do?'

'To a greater extent.'

'How then do you see the switch in the importance that it plays in your life?'

'You know, one of the problems of retirement is you need to engage your brain, you need to be busy or you die of boredom and depression. And poetry to some degree, not entirely, has taken up an empty space. Hence my desire to write this little book.'

'But isn't there something beyond that, in a more philosophical or psychological sense? After all, your work, as I said earlier, is quite metaphysical. You ask the big questions of meaning, and you probe in poem after poem, using irony, sometimes outright sarcasm, the foibles of human beings and our illusions.'

'I think I've always been like that to a degree. It goes back to my father and his atheism. There have always been the big issues: where do I fit into the universe, what is life? I'm very strong on evolution, for instance, as an aspect of spirituality rather than a god's creation. And now, in the retirement years it's just been more enhanced.'

'Are you writing a lot now?'

'I am writing a fair amount. And some of it is totally unphilosophical. I love the Johannesburg Art Gallery. I started going there when I was very young. I write a lot of poems about the art gallery.'

'Engaging with different art works?'

'And the internal architecture of the gallery, which I think is beautiful. Yes, the art works, all those things.'

'We should definitely include some of these new poems. But let's sort of round off and talk a little about the experience of doing this book.'

'Well, one of the generalities that has come out to me is how all these poets had early experiences with the 'Word'. You know, some of them you could call child geniuses. They were reading at age three, and stuff like that. The Word, and fascination with words and expressions, happened for most of them very, very early. And some others came out of homes where there wasn't that sort of stimulation but it happened to them, they were sort of waiting for it to happen, so it clicked in at school through good English teachers and stuff like that. Everybody's different. You know their poetry is different, but the one solid foundation is the love of the word and following from that, the literary intention.'

'Do you think interviewing the poets gave you a greater understanding of their work?'

'Not necessarily, but I certainly gained greater understanding of them as people. In some instances I went in blind, just talked to them without knowing their work well, or even knowing it at all. But there were some whose work I do know very well, for instance, Jane Fox. They were all fascinating interviews, particularly when it came to sitting down and transcribing them. I was fascinated by the voices and the intonations and the pauses that told me so much about them, and the laughter and the giggles that told me about the personalities. That was fascinating. And unfortunately I couldn't fully convey that in the transcripts without putting in little asides all over the bloody place. But having said that, I think including poems with the interviews will give the reader a better picture of where the work is coming from.'

I nod emphatically, 'Yes, they should. But to go back to an earlier point. You're a latecomer to poetry and now it's playing a very important part in your life which goes to show that the flame can be lit at any point. However, times change and many older poets bemoan the fact that it's difficult to find an audience, particularly for poetry that is less dramatic, but perhaps more intellectual, if that's the right term, than much of what they describe as performance poetry. Does this make you feel that what you're doing is just for self-gratification?'

'Recently people from Kensington have run gatherings at which I've read my work and I've had a very good response. That's been very pleasing. But, of course, writing has also been self-gratifying. I enjoy the process, starting off with a few words for an idea or two. Just like any other poet it sometimes takes weeks. I work on it and come back, and come back, and my wife plays a hell of a role in that. So self-gratification yes – the intellectual exercise.'

'Cecily is your first port of call for feedback?'

'And boy does she give feedback! She is so good on tone, brilliant my wife.'

'It's wonderful to have someone at your side.'

'Absolutely! And my wife is not intellectual, and she's not a poetry lover. But she'll look at something and she'll . . . ah.'

I laugh in acknowledgement. Theirs has certainly been an amazing marriage. I check the clock. The interview is running on past an hour; time for a final reflection.

'In say, fifty or a hundred years, how would you want someone to look back at your work? What should be the key element that they carry away from reading Mike Alfred's poetry?'

'What an incredibly difficult question. You are suggesting that I might have some posterity. I don't think so.'

'Your work might lie dormant for decades and then someone stumbles on it. That happens. What would be the elements that you would most want them to capture?'

'A sense of the irony of life, life without easy answers, life mixed with confusion and contradiction and puzzlement. I think those are the things that might come through in my poetry. And for which, yes, I'd like to be remembered. I don't see anything as being particularly simple or straightforward or ideal.'

'And stylistically, how do you see your work?'

'I've never thought in those terms, seriously. If you look at my poetry, you'll see a wide diversity of styles and approaches. Maybe the voice would be similar, the iconoclastic voice, the satirical voice. I don't rhyme much but I have written rhyming poetry. Lyric poetry, I don't know that I could call my stuff that. Descriptive poetry, yes, nature, yes, but I've never wanted to explore style. I've wanted to explore ideas.'

We both pause. Whew! Talk about the power and fascination of words! I switch off the tape-recorder. Plenty to work with here. Mike and I share a laugh. What have these two old codgers been rambling on about? The Divine Muse has surely touched us this evening . . .

□

This is a love poem written to my wife during the fiftieth year of our marriage.

Would you?

I don't believe in an after here.
I think you rot and disappear.
But were we offered eternity,
would you care to be with me?

This is a poem about the Johannesburg Art Gallery, which I've visited from the age of eight. I love the place and I enjoy many favourite artworks, including the life size bronze slave trembling in terror. And yes, I really do greet him by touching his shoulder.

The Statue in the Courtyard

I almost always greet him
with a touch to his bronze
shoulder. My father introduced
us when I was very young. His
emotions are so visible: hopelessness,
terror, helplessness, as he stands on
the auction floor in Salvador or perhaps
New Orleans, with prospective owners
appraising his beautiful, long muscled
utility. He has no idea that he's about
to establish great empires, great economies.
He knows that despite his magnificence,
life so far, has not treated him kindly.

☐

We overplay our own importance, no?

Buzz Aldrin

Buzz Aldrin,
a man of some perspective,
studied Earth when returning;
saw continents, seas, lakes and
snow clad mountains. Of humanity
there was no sign; all those billions,
all their clamour. Of man's great
kingdoms, there were no trace, from
out in space. Just Earth, cloud strewn,
serene, gorgeous, ancient as time. He
wondered whether Earth was greatly
influenced by man's dramatics, and
why man so forgetfully managed to
ignore ice ages, mass extinctions
and cosmic accidents?

I've written many poems attempting to capture the atmosphere of the city. This is one more. And it seems to be successful, as many expatriates have responded warmly.

Joeys

We're good chinas, Joeys and I.
We go back a long way, shared
birthdays for over 70 years. Joeys
knows he's a map inside my head,
a history pamphlet, and biographies.
We share the ever changing light
and thunder. We're buffeted by
August winds. We know there's just
enough water to float the flotilla of
rowboats on Zoo Lake. We know
where things are and where they were
and envisage what will be when I'm
gone. We know how to get to places:
six ways there and seven back. We
know when to go and where risk lurks.
And as for eating and drinking, our
heads spin. We know the roads, how
to avoid clowns and human missiles.
Beggars never get enough of us. We
intuit those invisible lines denoting
skin tones and income groups. We
note the blue clad devout on the hills,
and those called to mosque. Sirens
and too many crime stories we hear.
We help each other select razor wire.
We delight the Brazilian avenues and
listen when the birds sing thanks. Despite
problems, we're comfortable with one
another, Joeys and I; after all, it's home
territory, our meshing place. I know that
Joeys, my good mate, will be happy to
mix my ashes with his other allergens,
and please, don't forget the trams Joeys,
that wonderful time of trams.

□

David Webster lived nearby in Troyeville. I've always been fascinated by this extreme example of state instigated ferocity suddenly exploding in a sleepy suburb. It's taken me a long time, since his death to write it. [Oct 2013] It was prompted by a powerful, because peaceful, photograph of the man, in a visitor guide book.

Down

Once upon a beautiful, vicious morning,
a morning expectant both with innocence
and blood frenzy, the morning of the nod;
next job for the government psychopaths
watching from the blank hotel window.
They did not know why, did not care why,
only now, go! No one ever knew why, not
then, not yet. Down they drove in the
anonymous van, the van without plates,
without a driver, without a passenger and
down he went, shot full of shotgun gunshot,
down on the pavement where the boulder
remembers and the mosaic wall remembers
that bright Troyeville morning when no one
knew why they assassinated David Webster.
His official murderer doesn't remember
why or quite when or how he did it; he
doesn't remember much of himself at all.

☐

A poem written in the froth of our first election when the 'New SA' was truly new and we were truly hopeful.

Slovo's Short Freedom

Were those his best times,
walking alone in the sun
with his be-ribboned spaniel?
Walking again in the sun of
his youth, in the nostalgic
sun of his exile, and now
the glowing sun of fulfilment.
Basking in the warm space
of victory, under the blue Highveld
sky, old Johannesburg solid
wherever he looked. Home at
last, bearing the living hopes
of the dead and the dead
hopes of the living.

Yes, I think those were his
best times; before bodyguards,
before the elections, before the
clarion's demands wrung the
strength from his already
invaded frame. When he rejoiced
on sunny afternoons in Bez
Park, strolling, smiling at
strangers like me, snatching
those few warm minutes before
assuming the hopes of the
dead and the barely living.

☐

A few didactic intimations from the Master of the Universe

I can, said the creator, I can
offer, he said, only a life. Just
the spark to the starter motor,
a puff, a squeak and I'm done.
Life is all I can give you. Haven't
you realised that I'm an experimenter,
not an insurance salesman? So you
see, survival, survival is up to you;
it's your adventure. I can't guarantee
silk stockings, an apartment in Manhattan,
or pure intentions. But here's a word of
advice: don't put too much store in the words of
politicianseconomistsparentsteachersbossesexpertsbureaucratsmarketers,
they're purveyors of an obscene accumulation of
useless cant. And yes, if you press me, the
churches as well; far too powerful,
stronger than I. Isn't that something
now, stronger than god? Knocks all
your beliefs sideways doesn't it?
Sometimes I think I should have
become more directly involved.
Trouble is, I'm not all that sold on
morality. And anyway, running a
universe is one hell of a task. So as
I said, when the sperm docks with
the ovum, [hey, how's the space
age imagery?] my role is over.
My work ended when I got this evolution
thing working smoothly, well, more or less.
Allowed me to start tinkering with
other problems. There we are then,
that's my part of the deal: your life. And
there's one big advantage let me tell you,
you don't have to sign anything.

☐

We've often holidayed at Zinkwazi Beach just north of Stanger on the Kwazulu Natal North Coast. And I've written several poems about that green/blue world of cane fields and sea. This poem, with its attempt at strange rhyming, describes a holiday unusually wet, windy and overcast.

Grey

All week grey,
all the way to Tugela Mouth,
and beyond, and inland, and seaward, grey.
Day after day wet, with fierce winds; we take
grey walks on the brown, stinging beach, watching
the grey waves pound. A small hurricane today, the
bay a frothy white cauldron, with waves 'like those in
old shipwreck paintings,' says Cecily. Swimming and
surfing banned, to our dismay, Trees, with sturdy bend
and sway, do what they were bred for. Birds struggle
with force that doesn't ease their way. Rain as spray,
flies horizontal. We reach for another bottle of red,
open another thriller, great holiday.

□

An ironic, microscopic record of a small life.

A small biography . . .

and a short history
of a little fathering
and a little business
and a little poetry
and a little more than a little loving
and a little more wine thank you
and twenty three pairs of walking shoes
and much talk
and much thought
and a little action
and a little…
and a…
and…

Printed in the United States
By Bookmasters